East Lothian
Murder Chronicles

By

N. M. Lyons

Acknowledgements

Newspaper image © The British Library Board. All rights reserved. With thanks to The British Newspaper Archive (www.britishnewspaperarchive.co.uk).

In writing this book, I have been most grateful for the assistance given by a number of libraries and institutions. My thanks are particularly due to the National Library of Scotland, the John Gray Centre and the National Archives, Kew. To my family and friends, thank you for your continued support and encouragement.

For Mum and Dad,
the wisest of counsel.

Prologue

The county of East Lothian, previously known as Haddingtonshire, is an often-overlooked gem nestled in Scotland's central lowlands. Its boundaries include the Scottish Borders to the south, Edinburgh to the west and Midlothian to the south-west. The central administrative hub is the Royal Burgh of Haddington, which can trace its heritage back nine hundred years.

East Lothian is an area of extreme beauty that incorporates sweeping coastlines, dramatic topography, ancient monuments and historic settlements. The county's culture has been influenced at times by farming, large country estates, heavy industry and fishing. This book attempts to tap into this diversity and provide a flavour of East Lothian's criminal past by highlights different cases over several centuries. Some of the crimes are relatively well known, while others have been consigned to history. Such topics as witchcraft, mental illness, suicide, poisoning, misogyny, highway robbery, patricide and old-fashioned greed are visited.

N. M. Lyons
2021

Contents

Chapter 1

1570: The Three Clerics of Spott

Situated some two miles southwest of Dunbar is the community of Spott, bordered by the villages of Innerwick to the east and Stenton to the west. The area enjoys panoramic views of the Lammermuir Hills and the East Lothian coastline, while the parish's archaeology has helped chart the Roman occupation of southern Scotland. Moreover, Spott was featured in the first Battle of Dunbar in 1296, and the Scottish army camped at Doon Hill before their defeat by Oliver Cromwell's forces in the second Battle of Dunbar in 1650.

The area also has a rich social history, from the imposing Spott House, with its heritage dating back to the 13th century, to Spott Church, erected in 1790, which occupies an earlier Christian site. Further, a set of original 'Jougs', an iron collar yoke utilised for individuals who had incurred the kirk session's ire, is still in situ within the church boundaries. Significant landmarks in the area include 'The Witches Stone', located near where the Ringwood Witch, Marion Lillie, was put to death around 1698, and Spott Loan, which witnessed the witchcraft executions of October 1705.

Perhaps, though, the ecclesiastical narrative of this quiet rural parish during the 16th century offers the most perplexing and enduring tale of all. This intriguing trinity of cases begins with the murder of Robert Galbraith, a former parson of Spott who acted as treasurer and cleric of The Chapel Royal, Stirling. Galbraith ministered to James IV of Scotland's spiritual needs and was granted a legal charter in 1528, bestowing him lands near Berwick at Mydwyn Schelis in recognition of his service to the Crown.

As an advocate, he represented Queen Margaret Tudor, lodging his protests on her behalf in parliament on 1st September 1528, against any debts owed by Archibald Douglas, sixth Earl of Angus. Galbraith later became a Scottish Lord of Session and was inaugurated as one of the College of Justice's original senators on 7th November 1537. While overseeing a legal action in 1543, he was murdered by John Carkettle, a burgess of Edinburgh, and his associates, on account of preferential treatment afforded during legal action by the Law Lord to Sir William Sinclair of Hermanstoun. Although the murderers were apprehended and brought before parliament for their crimes, nothing is known of their fate.

Within our narrative, the second clergyman is Dr John Hamilton, the parson of Spott, who, in 1559, became an Archbishop and Scottish prelate during the reign of Mary, Queen of Scots. From an early age, Hamilton felt a religious calling and commenced his religious vocation at Paisley Abbey. In the years that followed, he furthered his education in Paris, and, on his return to Scotland, he rose to a position of power through the patronage of his brother James Hamilton, 2nd Earl of Arran and Regent of Scotland. John Hamilton became Keeper of the Privy Seal of Scotland in 1543 and Bishop of Dunkeld less than two years later.

As Archbishop of St Andrews, Hamilton made sustained efforts to forestall the spread of the Protestant faith in Scotland. Remaining an active partisan, he baptised James VI of Scotland and oversaw the divorce of Mary, Queen of

Scots, from Bothwell. However, the Archbishop was taken prisoner after a surprise night attack on Dumbarton Castle, which resulted in its annexation. He was quickly tried and found guilty for his 'art and part' in the deaths of Lord Darnley and Regent Moray. On 6th April 1571, Hamilton was hanged at the Mercat Cross, Stirling, just three days after his capture.

The case of our third Spott minister, John Kello, resonates most powerfully because of its focus on enmity and one man's quest for advancement at all costs. Originating from humble beginnings, Kello arrived at the parish of Spott as its first Protestant minister following the Scottish Reformation. He worked his way diligently through the church echelons, capably supported by his wife Margaret and their children, Bartilmo, Barbara and Bessie, and proved to be a popular figure within the parish.

Despite promising beginnings, Kello rapidly felt ill at ease, both with his financial situation, which consisted of a stipend of around 100 Scots pounds per annum, and a wife he considered to be curtailing his ambitions for professional and social advancement. After an initial financial investment proved fruitful, Kello speculated on properties in the Spott area; however, the expected returns failed to materialise, and he found himself further in debt.

Kello formulated a premeditated course of action, which centred upon a plan for his wife's death. Slowly but surely, he spread rumours amongst his parishioners that Margaret was prone to bouts of illness and fatalistic behaviour, before creating a will to provide for his family's financial future. In reality, as William Roughead noted in his 1913 treatise, *Twelve Scottish Trials*, Kello was 'preparing for his wife's death and a second marriage that would ensure his future advancement'.

Initially, he decided upon poison as his method of murder, but this proved ineffectual as Margaret had a strong physical constitution. Formulating a new stratagem, Kello invited several of his parishioners back to his home for a meal after his oration on 24th September 1570. On arrival, the front door was locked, and, receiving no answer to his knocks, Kello led the group to the back door and let himself in, embarking on a search for his wife.

On discovering Margaret dangling on a rope in a bedchamber, Kello cried out in anguish, 'My wife, my wife, my beloved wife is gone!' At first, the death was deemed a suicide, and parishioners quickly offered their sympathies, as stories swirled about Margaret's state of mind. However, Kello made a fatal mistake in the weeks before his wife's murder; he suffered a terrible fever, during which he had a vivid dream. Recounting this experience to Andrew Simpson, the visiting minister from Dunbar, he described facing a judge and fleeing from winged angels in the dream. In the wake of Margaret's death, the Dunbar minister remembered Kello's tale and decided that the dream represented the musings of a guilty mind.

When Kello visited Simpson some days after his wife's death, Simpson quickly accused Kello of murder and pleaded with him to acknowledge his crime. Conceding his guilt, Kello travelled to Edinburgh and convened fellow clergymen and a judge, to whom he admitted his culpability. He outlined his surreptitious entry to his wife's bedchamber while she was at prayer and told how he had taken a towel and strangled her. According to Kello's often convoluted prison confession, Margaret did not expire instantaneously and managed to forgive her husband's transgressions, saying that she would go to her grave happily if her passing could give 'vantage or pleasure' to his life.

It emerged that Kello had suspended his wife's lifeless body from a hook in the ceiling, setting the scene as if Margaret had hanged herself. Locking up the house and leaving from a back exit, he headed to the church and gave an impassioned sermon; an incredibly vibrant performance that impressed the congregation. An article in *Longman's Magazine* in February 1901 indicates that the effect was such that Kello's children sat, 'glowering at their father, feared like, for he was under a great gale'.

Upon Kello's confession of murder, the Edinburgh authorities were quick to pronounce judgement, decreeing that he should be hanged and his body burned. The verdict fitted with 16th-century standards of justice. Surprisingly, the Kello children were allowed an inheritance – a rarity, as his whole property should have been forfeited to the Crown. On 4th October 1570, at Gallow Lee, beside Leith Walk, and facing the scaffold, Kello uttered words of contrition to the assembled crowd, stating that, given his life over, he would have cherished and respected his wife. Moreover, within the prevailing climate of the time, he rebutted witchcraft rumours, vociferously maintaining to his death that he had never partaken in the 'wicked practices of the Magicians'.

Chapter 2

1612: Without Mercy

Scotland in the 17th century was a country largely censured by the state apparatus, which permeated every aspect of daily life. This autocratic structure was initiated after the Reformation of 1560, which resulted in the adoption of a Presbyterian system advancing ecclesiastical and secular court power. A code of conduct was utilised that covered nearly every eventuality, from simple local disputes to sexual misconduct and witchcraft – powers that exercised a form of social control, ensuring that the population lived God-fearing lives. The county of Haddingtonshire represented a microcosm of what was taking place throughout Scotland as kirk sessions, burgh courts, presbyteries and sheriff courts were interconnected through the rule of law.

It is perhaps therefore apt to use Margaret Alexander's case as an illustration of the judgemental and ruthless nature of Scottish society at this time. On a May morning in 1612, Margaret Alexander, a native of Aberlady, was taken before the sheriff court in Haddington, where she was charged with committing murder, incest and adultery. Before the court, the deposition outlined that Margaret was involved in an incestuous relationship for over seven years with a man named Patrick Learmouth, which produced two children.

Under the Scottish legal system of the time, the relationship was deemed incestuous as Patrick Learmouth was the widower of Margaret's sister, Marie. As a result, the charges were classified as a capital offence, carrying a mandatory death sentence if proven. The prosecution began by revealing the fate of the first child conceived during their relationship, asserting that Margaret attempted to induce an abortion after drinking some vile concoction that proved ineffective. It later emerged that Margaret recanted an earlier confession, where she claimed that another man named James Haitlie was the child's father.

Regardless of the lurid nature of the charges, the case was never going to be a well-balanced example of justice. The charges against Margaret Alexander were filtered through the kirk session of her home village of Aberlady and incorporated supposition from parishioners and church elders as much as any facts. Worse still for Margaret, she was a woman with grit, determination and a willingness to fight her case, demonstrating a level of tenacity sufficient to anger the assize.

While little information exists about the murder of the first child, the court supplies far greater detail relating to the second murder, which took place on 16th March 1612. The second child was allegedly conceived around the time when Margaret was called to appear before the Bishop of Dunkeld to answer charges of incest and infanticide. After this interview, it was specified to the court that Margaret continued her association with Peter Learmouth in Edinburgh, as the birth of her second child approached.

For the duration of Margaret's second pregnancy, Learmouth appears to have offered little or no support to the woman carrying his child. He advised Margaret to abort the child or pass the baby off as another man's if born. The case documents allude to Learmouth bringing Margaret back to his home in Aberlady, but, because of the kirk's regular searches of the village, Learmouth persuaded Margaret to flee to Haddington and carry out their plan.

Margaret Alexander then sought refuge at the house of her brother, William Lauder, in Haddington, and gave birth at his brewhouse on 19th March 1612. Margaret was accused of murdering her child, hiding the dead body under her clothing, and travelling on an errand to the nearest port with her niece. Dispatching her companion on a false undertaking, she, 'gaid to the dyk side beside the watter' and, 'with [her] handis, laid the bairne in the same and coverit it with the muddis of the dyke, and there left it and came hame'.

Margaret moved to a ditch by the edge of the water and buried the dead infant in the mud before journeying back to her brother's home. However, the child was discovered. Rather than receiving a Christian burial, the dead child was laid out at the Mercat Cross. These actions by the authorities were to showcase Margaret's perverted and unnatural acts of motherhood. Fearing for her life, she journeyed to Aberlady to be reunited with Peter Learmouth, who sent her on horseback to the Port of Leith.

At this juncture of the case, the full might of the Church and court was brought to bear as the nature of Margaret and Peter's relationship was revisited, and a moral judgement was duly pronounced. As she had committed infanticide, an act that would almost certainly guarantee a guilty verdict from the jury, Margaret was expelled from the Church. The charges levelled against her demonstrate the full remit and secular court power of the Presbyterian Church in Scotland. Parishioners, clergy and court officials viewed the acts carried out by Margaret not as crimes but as affronts to the moralistic and religious society of the time.

When Margaret answered for her crimes, she openly admitted to them all, except the murder of her newborn children. Despite her protestations of innocence, the court was quick to return a guilty verdict on all points of the case – a unanimous decision, declared by the assize chancellor, David Forrest. In line with Scots law, the guilty verdict ensured that Margaret Alexander would face the hangman's noose for capital crimes. However, this was not a process formulated around justice; instead, it debased a broken woman who did not receive a fair trial.

The trial judge or 'dempster' of the court, William Sinclair, declared that Margaret Alexander would be sentenced in two parts. First, she would face a public shaming as a forewarning to others as she was, 'takin furth of this tolbuith and in exemplarie maner to hir reproche and schame', before ultimately being executed, with her corpse openly displayed.

Margaret Alexander endured a highly structured punishment, as part of which she was taken from Haddington Tolbooth and made to confess to her crimes at the brewhouse and the kirkyard. Further, she was forced to dig up the dead body of her child using only her bare hands in the presence of her fellow parishioners. A sight like this is abhorrent to our modern mindset, but, in an era of public executions where it was common to spectate while women were strangled and burned as witches, it was deemed an appropriate punishment. Margaret then faced the scaffold at the Mercat Cross, Haddington. After her hanging, both her arms were cut off below the elbow – one was displayed at the North Port entrance to Haddington and the other in Aberlady.

This case cannot be explored in terms of criminal charges; after all, over 400 years have passed since. Instead, the life and death of Margaret Alexander offer a window into an early modern Scottish society in which church and state set down the parameters of acceptable behaviour. Guilty or innocent, Margaret Alexander stood no chance of facing the genuine scales of justice. The patriarchal society of Scotland in 1612 depended on social control, the collusion of church and state and their power to degrade, maim and kill in the name of the greater good.

Chapter 3

1629: A Condemned Woman

Haddingtonshire can trace its origins to the High Middle Ages and the 12th century kingdom of King David I of Scotland. The area has borne witness to several medieval and early modern conflicts. Over the centuries that followed, the diverse landscape and skilled workforce have helped support an eclectic range of industries from agriculture and coal mining to fishing and textile production. The chemical, glass and ceramic industries that operated along the coastal shoreline and the wire mills of Musselburgh helped to establish the region's national importance.

Unfortunately, a distressing and brutal side has also existed to life within the county, perhaps manifested most strikingly in the 16th and 17th century witch hunts. Among the most infamous events of this era were the North Berwick Witch Trials in 1590, which lasted for over two years and implicated over 70 people. As late as 1705, long after witch trials had been forcefully discredited elsewhere, many witches were burnt to death at Spott Loan. The only certainty afforded to these individuals was torture and, if found guilty, a truly macabre and horrific ending to their lives.

Of the many names that echo down the generations, perhaps that of Isobel Young offers one of the most complete stories. Born around 1565 in East Barns, Isobel was blessed by the standards of the day. She had made a perfect marriage to George Smith, who was an elite member of local society. He was titled a 'portioner', which is to say that he enjoyed the right to work a portion of land under a heritable system, thus enabling him to buy or sell the land with the permission of his feudal superior, to whom he would also owe an annual 'feu duty' – a payment either in cash or in kind.

Over the course of Isobel's married life, she raised a large family and enjoyed the benefits of living on a smallholding, raising livestock, farming land and employing staff members. Nevertheless, Isobel possessed a fiery character and was known for arguing with her neighbours – not ideal behaviour in a rural community where petty jealousy or economic competition could precipitate one person denouncing another as a witch.

In Isobel's case, she came under investigation by the Dunbar Presbytery in 1624 when two local women, Margaret Melrose and Janet Acheson, under interrogation, named her as a woman with a reputation for practising witchcraft. In April 1624, both women, as well as two others, named Margaret Baxter and Marion Bathgate, provided testimony. Regrettably, no legitimate proof is available from the presbytery's records to quantify events, and, although Isobel was discharged, these events tarnished her reputation.

In the five years that elapsed between her first and second tribunals, Isobel gained a higher level of notoriety in the parish, and the authorities became more zealous in their investigations of her. By 1629 the case against Isobel Young centred around four different witchcraft conventions. It was alleged that she had consorted with witches and the devil, partaken in the financial destruction of her enemies, inflicted disease on others and transferred illness to another individual. Isobel faced 24 charges of witchcraft centred upon threats, curses and malicious acts related to money, land and petty local disputes.

On 13th January 1629, Isobel entered the Tolbooth prison in Edinburgh to prepare for her trial. However, when the date passed without action, she wrote to the Council to complain about her treatment. In her letter, she openly accused her enemies of trying to keep her in the squalid conditions of the Tolbooth for an indefinite period, circumstances which were especially frightening to a woman of over 80 years of age.

By the time the indictment against Isobel Young began in February 1629, she had fought an uphill struggle for freedom. As we have seen previously, the Presbyterian Kirk wielded enormous power in Scotland and influenced a highly superstitious public into believing that witches were omnipresent and the source of evil and misfortune. Moreover, Isobel had spent several decades cultivating an image centred upon witchcraft. In a Scottish coastal community in the 17th century, this would have imbued her with a daunting reputation. Isobel's connections to acknowledged witches, including Janet Lindsay and Katharine Gray, executed at Haddington, as well as to her accusers, Margaret Melrose and Janet Acheson, added further weight to the charges proffered against her.

The crown's case was bolstered by members of the community who chronicled their interactions with her. Andrew Morton indicated that, when Isobel requested a debt settlement, which he could not pay, she recoiled and uttered 'most blasphemous words' against him. Subsequently, his wife encountered the accused at the local kirk, where Isobel allegedly threatened the Morton family with the loss of all their worldly possessions – an outcome that came to pass.

The prosecution was aware of the need for impartial proof as Isobel had failed to confess to any charges. They claimed that she carried the 'Devil's mark' on her body, located under her left breast. Isobel would testify that this was an ulcer that had developed several years earlier, but Mr Alexander Fortune, who ministered to the wound, detailed that it appeared to give the patient no pain and that, even after his best efforts, it had never healed. This testimony strengthened the case against Isobel as the 'Devil's mark' was known as the permanent mark of the Devil on his servants, sealing their obedience to him and created by the raking of his claw across their flesh or by branding in blue or red using a hot iron.

The defence case acted outside the traditional parameters of a 17th century witch trial. By 1629 three of Isobel's sons were married with children of their own. One was a portioner in his own right, enabling the family to continue to thrive financially. Isobel's apparent wealth and social standing meant that she could make use of professional legal counsel at her trial – at the time of rebuttal, she had two advocates and her sons representing her interests.

The defence strategy was to argue that there was a complete absence of witchcraft in the case put forward by the prosecution: 'There were no witnesses to magical deeds, and without tangible proof of such events, such pronouncements were ridiculous.' The integrity of particular witness testimony was cast into doubt, and it was maintained that, rather than casting supernatural curses against people, Isobel was simply an older woman venting her emotions on a situation in which she felt aggrieved. Without a doubt, it emerges that Isobel was capable of issuing threats, guarding her family's prosperity vigorously, but this was not a case based on witchcraft. Instead it represented a statement of cultural and socio-economic concerns involving a small community at odds with each other and the place of women in a society where power was related to privilege.

Isobel faced damning testimony from friends and neighbours she had known throughout her long life. Worse still, her own husband testified against her. Many of the witnesses could never have reasoned that they would have to appear before the justiciary in Edinburgh, let alone be given the freedom to change or recant their testimony. Ultimately, Isobel was cleared of half the charges against her – nonetheless, the jury found her guilty of witchcraft, which was punishable by death. The judge duly pronounced the sentence, and Isobel Young was taken to Castle Hill, Edinburgh, and strangled at the stake. Her body was burned to ashes.

Isobel's story demonstrates that her family's high social standing within her community did not prevent her from being denounced as a witch. Did she face torture, intimidation or sleep deprivation as the authorities tried to gain a confession? We can only guess, but, because it was alleged that Isobel carried the Devil's mark on her body, the general course of action was pricking. This technique involved inserting a needle or pin into the mark to examine its sensitivity. Bleeding or lack of pain demonstrated that the suspect was a witch. However, Isobel never faltered in her protestations of innocence, in defiance of the treatment that she must have faced. Ultimately, this case and countless others like it were orchestrated by the social elite rather than the authorities succumbing to the clamour of the general public. The culpability for these terrible crimes against Isobel and women like her lies with the kirk sessions, which began the investigations, and the secular court that prosecuted them at trial.

Chapter 4

1688: Ordeal by Touch

Sir James Stansfield was very much a man of his time; born in Yorkshire in the 17th century, he proved to be both adept on the battlefield and, later, in the business world. During the English Civil War, James Stansfield gained a commission in the Parliamentarian army and acted as secretary to Major General Morgan. After Cromwell's success at the Battle of Dunbar in 1650, Colonel Stansfield migrated north to Scotland and set up a linen and wool manufacturing business at Newmilns in the parish of Haddington, under the protectorate of the newly establish Commonwealth.

Following the Restoration in 1660, Charles II conferred a knighthood on Stansfield for his commercial success despite his previous republican allegiance. This recognition attracted financial support from the government, thus enabling him to expand his business ventures. Unfortunately, these achievements could not be replicated in his personal life. His marriage faltered and he had strained relationships with his sons, Philip and John. Despite the benefits of a good family upbringing and a liberal education, the siblings developed antecedent tendencies in adulthood.

John was a profligate, and his older brother Philip was far worse, with villainous and debauched tendencies that saw him imprisoned in Antwerp, Orleans and the notorious Marshalsea Prison at Southwark, south of the River Thames. Philip Stansfield despised his father and his relationship with his mother excited lurid gossip within society. Accordingly, Sir James found it impossible to find any shred of genuine humanity in his son's character and decided to disinherit him in favour of his brother John. Hearing this revelation, Philip Stansfield openly declared to friends that he would slit his father's throat.

On 27th November 1687, Sir James Stansfield shared a convivial meal with his friend, the Rev. John Bell, who would later describe James as 'calm, rational and [in] reasonably good cheer'. At the end of the evening, Bell went to the guest room, but the minister awoke to the sound of raised voices, leading him to believe that there were 'evil spirits about that house that night'. This assertion proved to be judicious, as Sir James had disappeared from the house.

Later that same day, a man travelling by a pool of water near the Stansfield property was chilled by the sight that confronted him. Philip Stansfield was crouched down at the edge of the pool, transfixed by something floating in the water – the dead body of his father. Philip was quick to maintain that Sir James had been suffering from exhaustion and had committed suicide while his mental faculties were impaired. Ever the loving son, he declared that his father had 'died like a beast.' Within an hour, he had secured all the valuables belonging to Sir James and, in a pyrrhic victory, placed his father's silver shoe buckles on his own feet.

This behaviour galvanised friends of the deceased to contact the Lord Advocate, who agreed that Sir James Stansfield's death warranted further investigation. He ordered the body to be examined for any signs of criminal violence. However, Philip seized the communication in transit, allowing him to organise an expedient funeral. The Lord Advocate was enraged by this behaviour and ordered the body to be exhumed for a full post-mortem.

After the examination, the surgeons requested that Philip help them to place his father's body back into his coffin. These actions instigated the ancient ritual known as the 'ordeal by touch', whereby if a murder suspect touched the corpse and caused it to bleed, he was guilty. When Philip raised his father's head, blood began to emanate from Sir James's neck, horrifying his son and causing him to faint – thus sealing his guilt in the eyes of the onlookers.

Philip Stansfield was arrested and jailed at Edinburgh's Tolbooth in anticipation of his trial, which began on 7th February 1688, on a charge of treason against the Crown, the wilful murder of his father and libel. Representing the prosecution, Sir John Dalrymple argued that Philip Stansfield had recruited several cohorts to his cause. The prosecution asserted that the mistress of the accused, Janet Johnston, in collusion with the accused's friend George Thomson, known as 'the Devil's tailor', and Thomson's wife Helen Dickson, had aided in the murderous plot.

After a lightning opening to the prosecution, Dalrymple found it incredibly difficult to fashion a case based on this hypothesis. Philip Stansfield's alleged accomplices would not provide incriminating testimony and continued to maintain their innocence, despite having endured the crippling pain of a 'thumbikin' – an instrument of torture involving compressing the thumb. The same means of torture was used on Sir James's servants to no avail. As none of these individuals incriminated themselves, no charges could be issued.

Notwithstanding these setbacks to the case, 13-year-old James Thomson and Janet Johnston's 10-year-old daughter Anna Mack provided more illuminating details. While the court refuted the children's testimony because of their young age, the jury insisted that they should be permitted to declare what they knew about the events surrounding the murder. James indicated that, on the evening of the murder, Philip Stansfield had arrived at the home of his father, George Thomson, in the company of Janet Johnston. He maintained that Philip threatened to kill Sir James and confirmed that he 'would be obliged to the Thomas family when he had inherited the family estate'. Around eleven o'clock in the evening, Philip and Janet departed. James's parents followed them later. On his parents' return some two hours later, James heard his father tell his mother that 'the deed was done'.

On the night of the murder, Anna Mack established that Philip Stansfield had visited her family home and instructed her to find out whether Sir James had returned from Edinburgh. Confirming that Sir James was at Newmilns, Philip left the house with her mother, Janet. Later that evening, Anna's father instructed her to bring her mother home. Anna found that her mother was with Philip Stansfield at George Thomson's house and pleaded with her to come home. Her mother did not return until two o'clock in the morning, when Anna heard her seething father ask his spouse, 'Bitch and whore, where have you been for so long?' Janet shot back, 'The deed is done!'

Even with these damning statements, the prosecution's case hinged on the testimony of the surgeon James Muirhead, who carried out the post-mortem. He detailed to the court that 'a large and conspicuous swelling' had been discovered on the side of the subject's dislocated neck, but there were no other injuries, and water had not been present in his lungs. In Muirhead's opinion, these findings were concurrent with a death caused by manual strangulation and not drowning.

Muirhead outlined that Sir James's neck was bleeding as the accused helped lift the body into his coffin. The corpse had been sewn up and encased in fresh, clean linen, and no blood had been visible before Philip Stansfield handled the deceased. With a sense of triumph, the Crown prosecution described this action as 'the Divine Majesty, who loves to see just things done legally' furnishing 'full probation in an extraordinary manner'.

Faced with almost insurmountable odds, the defence counsel led by Sir Patrick Hume interceded, postulating that the 'ordeal by touch' was 'a superstitious observation, founded neither upon law nor reason'. This observation failed to carry weight with the jury in proving Philip Stansfield's innocence in his father's murder. In addition, the accused was charged with treason, accused of drinking a toast against the king. However, the defence argued that Philip Stansfield was, in fact, an ardent supporter of the king, having volunteered as a soldier in the Earl of Dumbarton's regiment in the fight against the Monmouth rebellion. For the charge of libel, which declared that Philip Stansfield had previous convictions and had openly threatened his father's life and engaged in trying to kill his father on hearing of his disinheritance, these arguments were classified as hearsay and fabrications that had been brought forward to blacken the character of the accused.

As to the indictment of patricide, the defence put forward a plea that Philip Stansfield was innocent of this charge and went to bed early on the evening in question. Philip was awoken by Sir James's servant the following morning, who informed him that the master of the house was missing. Upon hearing this information, the accused quickly got dressed, but received a message informing him of his father's death.

The defence case was centred solely on the proposition that Sir James had drowned himself while mentally deficient. However, the medical evidence, the children's statements and the 'ordeal by touch', admitted into a Scottish trial for the very last time, refuted this. As the prosecution acidly observed, the notion that 'after Sir James had strangled himself and broken his neck he then drowned himself strained belief.' Ultimately, Philip Stansfield was doomed by the failure of even a single witness to appear on his behalf.

As the trial came to an end, an oddity emerged – perhaps not a complete shock given the utilisation of the 'ordeal by touch' and thumbscrews during the proceedings. As the jury retired to deliberate a verdict, the Lord Advocate ordered 'an assize of error against the inquest' should Stanfield be acquitted. This meant that if any member of the jury decided to free the defendant, they would be fined and imprisoned for a 'wilful error'.

Of course, this was never going to be an issue. Philip Stansfield was unanimously found guilty of high treason, libel for cursing his father, and, finally, a distinctly Scottish legal charge defined as 'murder under trust' – murdering someone who has shown confidence in them, such as a parent, sibling, child, or even servant.

The Lords, Justice General and Commissioners of Justiciary decreed that Philip Stansfield would forfeit all his lands and goods for high treason against the Crown. On 15th February, he was taken to the Mercat Cross, Edinburgh, and hanged in a gibbet until he died. His tongue was cut out and burnt upon a scaffold, and his right hand cut off and nailed to the East Port Gate of Haddington. His bodily remains were then taken to the Gallow Lee – the midway point between Edinburgh and Leith – and placed in chains.

Philip Stansfield's final moments proved to be torturously painful – the noose loosened around his throat during the hanging, forcing the executioner to strangle him by hand. A formal request for a Christian burial was denied, and Stansfield's body was left to hang in chains. However, the corpse was removed and later found face down in water. In the end, Philip Stansfield's state execution almost exactly mirrored his father's murder; for some, the eerie similarity was poetic justice, while for others it was shockingly macabre.

Chapter 5

1795: The Malady of Major Kinloch

East Lothian is home to some of the most remarkable medieval castles in Scotland, yet the county is also strongly associated with large working estates and country residences. One of the most significant of these properties is Gilmerton House, which nestles between Athelstaneford and East Linton, representing a splendid example of Georgian architecture. Commissioned by Sir David Kinloch, the 5th baronet, the Grade A property was built by John Aitken in the 1750's and extended by William Burns in 1828, and it remains the Kinloch family's seat to this day.

One of the most notable family members was Major Alexander Gordon Kinloch, born around 1749 to Sir David Kinloch, fifth Baronet of Gilmerton, and his wife Harriet Cockburn, daughter of Archibald Cockburn, a highly respected Scottish advocate. Kinloch embarked on a military career at an early age, serving as an Ensign in the Royal Irish Regiment before rising to the rank of Captain by 1778, in which role he was stationed at Coxheath, Nova Scotia.

Kinloch proved an exemplary officer and gained further promotion to the rank of Major in 1779, setting sail with his regiment for the West Indies. During his time in St Lucia, Major Kinloch contracted a fever, which decimated many of his fellow soldiers – some 1,800 men perished out of a company of 5,000. Although Kinloch did recover, his disposition underwent a marked change.

By the autumn of 1789, Major Kinloch had returned to Scotland. Soon, his behaviour began to concern his family and several incidents displayed an irrational mindset. His actions were so out of step with society that he was consigned to a stay in Edinburgh's Bedlam, although no exact date for this can be confirmed. In the months preceding his father's death in 1795, Major Kinloch struck his older brother Francis at the dining table, wounding him badly, although it appears that the outburst was resolved amicably.

When his father, Sir Francis, the 5th Baronet, died on 18th February 1795, Major Kinloch was dissatisfied with his inheritance of 1,300 pounds – some 200 pounds less than he had expected. Two months later, he shot and killed his older brother, thus beginning a chain of events that would lead to an innovative Scottish criminal trial.

The subsequent legal contest set out the future parameters for the use and validity of notes taken by witnesses as testimony. More importantly, this trial represents one of the first recorded verdicts of diminished responsibility as a result of mental instability, although this terminology was never formally utilised at the trial. The legal process got underway before the High Court of Justiciary on Monday 29th June 1795, with Lord Justice Clerk, Lord Braxfield, acting as the presiding judge. Robert Dundas of Arniston led the prosecution, while David Hume led Major Kinloch's defence team. The jury consisted of 15 local 'gentleman' led by Andrew Wauchope[1] of Niddrie Marischal House.

---

[1] Andrew Wauchope was part of the family that owned the Niddrie Marischal Estate until the 20th century.

Major Kinloch entered the court when it was not yet ten o'clock in the morning dressed sombrely in black, reflecting his demeanour. It was acknowledged that Sir Archibald Gordon Kinloch had been arrested for the murder of his brother, Sir Francis Kinloch, 6th Baronet,[2] either on the evening of 14th April 1795 or in the early hours of the following morning. The charge stated that the murder had taken place at Gilmerton House and that Major Kinloch had submitted a plea of not guilty. One of the most significant witnesses to appear was George Somner, a surgeon from the market town of Haddington. Under examination from the Solicitor General, Mr Blair revealed that he was well acquainted with the Kinloch family. On Monday 13th April 1795, Somner received a message from Miss Harriet Kinloch asking him to travel to Gilmerton House immediately.

On arrival, Mr Somner indicated to the court that he had learned from Miss Kinloch of her wish for him to dissuade her brother, Major Gordon Kinloch, from travelling to Edinburgh. As Mr Somner entered the house, he noticed the gentleman sitting in the corner and indicated to the court that, at that time, he believed that the Major was quite mad and should not be allowed to leave the house. Somner detailed to the court that he had shared his views with Miss Kinloch and her eldest brother, Sir Francis Kinloch.

On the following day, Mr Somner asserted that he was requested to journey back to Gilmerton House as a matter of urgency and bring the 'necessary equipment'. For the benefit of the court', Mr Somner clarified that he understood this request to mean that he should bring a straitjacket with him. He journeyed with haste to Gilmerton House with a trained

---

[2] Major Kinloch somewhat ironically inherited the Baronet title after killing his brother.

nurse in attendance, arriving at ten o'clock in the evening. On entering the property, he asked for help from the servants to shackle Major Kinloch, but none were able or willing to do so.

The Lord Advocate interceded at this point in the examination and asked Mr Somner, 'Did you see the Major out of his room at any time before he came down to the parlour that evening?' Mr Somner indicated to the court that he had been alerted to the Major's presence at the top of the stairs between one and two o'clock in the morning, wearing only his breeches and shirt. Recommencing his questioning, the Solicitor General ascertained from the witness that he had endeavoured to calm the situation and took hold of the Major's arms to escort him back to bed, but the Major drew a pistol from the pocket of his breeches. On hearing the disturbance, Sir Francis appeared and asked his brother Gordon, 'What is the matter?'

He replied, 'I do not know what to do. I am ill, and I cannot sleep.' Mr Somner indicated that, at about three o'clock that same morning, Major Kinloch rose from his bed and came back down to the parlour. When he returned to his room, Somner and Sir Francis followed the Major. A confrontation ensued on the staircase, and Mr Somner indicated that he witnessed a flash of light and a pistol report. Sir Francis exclaimed, 'I am done for.' Mr Somner helped Sir Francis back to his room and, upon removing his shirt, found a wound some three or four inches below the breastbone. Sir Francis was laid in bed, confiding that he had acted foolishly in trying to seize his brother.

Although the bullet had traversed through the body of Sir Francis, Dr Benjamin Bell managed to extract it from his backbone, close to the spine. Despite the success of this delicate procedure, however, Sir Francis died on the evening of 16th April 1795, some 44 hours after being shot. Sir Francis's death bed wish was for the authorities not to be involved, but Major Kinloch was put under arrest and transported to Haddington Jail that very day. On 18th April 1795, George Somner, Dr Benjamin Bell and James Horne of Edinburgh officially certified the death. However, there is no clear indication in the records of why this post-dated the death by some 36 hours. Major Kinloch was transferred to the Tolbooth Jail in Edinburgh on 24th April 1795, and his pistols, inscribed with the name of their maker, H.W. Mortimer of London, were passed over as evidence along with the pistol ball extracted from the dead body.

In the remainder of his testimony, Mr Somner intimated to the court that he did not see Major Kinloch again until he was at Haddington Jail. At this time, Mr Goldie, the minister from Athelstaneford, was also in attendance and informed the accused that it was beholden upon him to direct the affairs of Gilmerton House. Major Kinloch replied that he was in no state of mind to answer questions relating to this. Mr Goldie and the Sheriff Clerk, Mr Fraser, were appointed to act on the Major's behalf, with his agreement.

Over the course of the Crown's case, 13 witnesses, including family, friends and servants from Gilmerton House offered their testimonies. They all confirmed that Major Kinloch had exhibited signs of insanity, but not all of the medical witnesses who took to the stand shared this opinion.

One of the most exciting testimonies was that of Charles Hay, Sir Francis Kinloch's solicitor. He provided details of private conversations between the two men that took place both in a professional capacity and between friends. Noting to the court that he had last seen Sir Francis in early March, Charles Hay intimated that the deceased had gone through his father's papers on inheriting the baronet title. Major

Kinloch believed that his elder brother had destroyed family documents – a process he considered to be detrimental to the prospects of younger family members, including himself.

Mr Hay formulated a written legal opinion in which he indicated his belief that the financial settlement provided to the younger members of the Kinloch family was more than generous and exceeded the legal requirements for this, meaning that it did not require further legal investigation. This outcome was a factor in the Major's initial attack on his older brother, although the Major also had delusions that his brother was attempting to poison him with pills.

The exculpatory submission came from Lieutenant Colonel Samuel Twentyman of Lincoln, who was examined under oath by Mr Hume. Noting to the court that he first made the acquaintance of Major Kinloch in 1778, he certified that, during their military careers, 'no officer was more universally esteemed' and his 'generosity, good temper, sociability and general good conduct made him extremely popular both in his own and other regiments'. In his testimony, Colonel Twentyman revealed that, on the island of St Lucia between 1779 and 1780, Major Kinloch had contracted a terrible fever that deprived him of his common sense. Twentyman noted that his comrade had been 'confined to bed in a state of delirium'.

Mr Hume requested further information on the treatment of the accused, which the Colonel readily supplied to the courtroom. Major Kinloch was moved to Barbados for a change of air and to heighten his chances of recovery. Lieutenant Fawcett, then stationed in India, accompanied the patient on his passage. He later conveyed to Colonel Twentyman that Major Kinloch's servant contracted the same illness and, in a paroxysm, threw himself overboard and was drowned. Mr Hume interjected and asked if there had been any significant changes in the character of the accused. Twentyman recalled that, on meeting Major Kinloch on his return to Europe and on subsequent occasions in the intervening years, manifest change in his behaviour was apparent.

Twentyman confirmed that this change was evident 'not in terms of his outward appearance, but from a total alteration in his conduct, manners, and conversation'. In his closing attestation, Colonel Twentyman reasserted that he had no doubt that the fever had altered Major Kinloch's character and that the periodic attacks from which he suffered had rendered him insane and unable to control his actions.

Major John Mackay, who had been on friendly terms with the accused since the inception of their military careers, supplied further corroboration of this to the trial. He recounted to the court that he had met the Major at many social occasions over the years and had found that his personality swayed from perfect civility to a deep melancholic state. Under examination from Mr Rae, Major Mackay detailed his encounter with the accused at Dumbreck Hotel, Edinburgh, in the days after the death of Kinloch's father. He declared that the Major appeared 'to be depressed in his mind and quite incoherent in what he said'. Although he extolled his brother's virtues and indicated that he was happy with his inheritance, a repetition of questions was necessary to elicit an answer.

Major Mackay then advised the court that, on returning home, he told his sister that he would not be surprised if Major Kinloch had 'not committed some rash act against himself'. Drawing on the point relating to Major Kinloch's coherence during their meeting, the Lord Advocate asked the witness if the accused was capable of giving a rational and distinct answer to a question at that time. Major Mackay reiterated his early observation that, while the Major was lucid, he conversed with a 'degree of melancholy and wildness, which I had never observed before'.

As the Lord Advocate drew the trial to a close, he indicated to the bench, 'Gentleman, the question you are to determine comes to this short and simple issue. If it appears that the accused was in a situation of knowing good from evil, then you cannot acquit him.' The jury's deliberations returned a unanimous judgement of guilty on 15th July 1795, although Major Kinloch (referenced during the trial as the 'pannel') was declared insane and thus not an object of punishment. Saved from the death penalty, Major Kinloch was sentenced to life imprisonment and summarily confined to Edinburgh's Tolbooth Jail.

However, an odd addendum to the sentence allowed anyone to secure Major Kinloch's release with a settlement of 10,000 pounds sterling. An undertaking had to be entered into with the court to hold Major Kinloch securely in another place (almost an 18th-century form of house arrest) for this to take place. Less than two days later, Dr William Farquharson, whose Crown testimony had focused on Major Kinloch's mental state and use of laudanum, approached Lord Braxfield and successfully secured Kinloch's release into his care.

Dr Farquharson's intercession on behalf of Major Kinloch drew the case to a close, yet the question remains whether the verdict was just and fair. The Major undoubtedly suffered a debilitating illness in St Lucia – most likely yellow fever or 'yellow jack', so named because of the associated jaundice observed in many patients. This could, in turn, have progressed to encephalitis, which would corroborate the manifest change in Major Kinloch's personality –

encephalitis can lead to cognitive changes that alter a person's emotional and behavioural attitudes, resulting in depression and mood disorders, which were not medically understood at the time but were important for the trial's findings. While Major Kinloch took up residence with Dr Farquharson at his home at World's End Close[3] on the Royal Mile in Edinburgh, the good doctor disappears from official records. As for the 7th Baronet, he died less than five years later, ostensibly, we must surmise, in Farquharson's home, as per the legal requirements of the case.

---

[3] A 'close' is a generic term used in Scotland to denote the entrance of a private property entrance, whereas a 'wynd' is an open thoroughfare, usually wide enough for a horse and cart. The 'World's End Close' references the fact that it sat just inside the 'Netherbow Gate' – the entrance to Edinburgh's city wall. Residents who could not afford the entrance fee back into the city stayed their whole lives within the confines of the city walls.

Chapter 6

1808: The Footpad Thief

The romanticised idea of the outlaw is commonplace in the annals of Scottish history, especially in the wake of Sir Walter Scott's publication of *The Heart of Midlothian* (1818), the seventh in his series of Waverley novels, which immortalises the story of a heroine waylaid by highwaymen. The reality of the outlaw life was far less glamorous, however, and involved crimes perpetrated by means of acts of violence, interrupting the smooth transportation of money, travellers and merchandise.

During the 18th century, two types of robbers were looking for suitable targets. Mounted horsemen known as 'knights of the road' enjoyed a certain level of prestige with the public, but 'urban footpads' or street thieves were deemed far more dangerous. The highwayman would ply his trade on main roads to and from cities and in open countryside, whereas the footpad thief was more likely to accost their prey on city streets, often late at night.

Traditional representations of highwaymen centre upon England, but ample evidence exists that robbers operated just as effectively in Haddingtonshire. The Great North Road, which linked Edinburgh to London, passed through the county, as well as countless small thoroughfares. The major transportation arteries would have seen bustling stagecoaches conveying people around the county, and the evolving mail service used mail coaches to transport letters and parcels. Such was the mail service's success that, by 1797, 42 routes were in operation across Britain, linking most of the major cities.

Unfortunately, as late as the mid-18th century, smaller road tracks in the region could be challenging to traverse in the winter months. Despite the obligation of rural communities to maintain these routes through the 'statue labour' system – a commitment undertaken by local landowners and tenants to supply the necessary workforce – this arrangement was fraught with inconsistencies and corruption. Not until the advent of the turnpike system could a road be effectively maintained and upgraded by levying a toll on its users. When the fragility of its transportation infrastructure is contemplated in conjunction with the large numbers of lone, vulnerable travellers passing through the region, Haddingtonshire offered tantalising opportunities to prospective robbers.

Accordingly, despite the myriad of cases that shed light upon highway robbery in Haddingtonshire for this narrative, the focus will not be on the traditional highwayman but instead on the errant footpad thief. The case of James Holland is of particular interest, not because of the audacity of the crime – it was a simple case of robbery with violence – but because it demonstrates how a footpad thief could operate in a rural location and the severity of the court judgement that his activities attracted.

When James Holland appeared before the High Court of Justiciary in Edinburgh on Monday 12th December 1808, the private soldier of the 6th (Inniskilling) Dragoons, a cavalry regiment that had distinguished itself at the Battle of the

Boyne in 1690, found himself in a precarious situation. On 18th November 1808, Holland encountered John Hay, a tenant from Duncanlaw, Yester, on the Gifford road, about a mile from Haddington. Holland allegedly jumped out of his hiding place and boldly seized the bridle of his subject's horse, before ordering Hay to hand over his money, threatening to blow out his brains if he refused to do so.

The first witness to appear before the court was Mr John Hay, who established that, on the night in question, he had departed The Bell Inn, Haddington at just after five o'clock in the afternoon following an earlier visit to the local market. At that time, he was with James Cunningham, James Hay and William Simpson. The four men became separated at Nungate Bridge, and John Hay and James Cunningham journeyed on ahead to Yester. As they continued their journey, they saw two men run past them, but, as the afternoon light had faded, they could not distinguish their features.

After riding on for about half a mile, the witness was stopped by an assailant, who grabbed his horse's bridle and demanded money in a threatening manner. Hay replied, 'that he was surely joking' and refused to acquiesce, even with the threat of death. Holland then struck him a blow to the head with a bludgeon, causing Hay to fall from his horse. On recovering from the attack, Hay found himself flat on his back and the robber dragging him along the road, making several attempts to drag him into the adjoining field.

Unable to do this, the robber sprang backwards and put his hands up to his quarry's coat, on the right side where his watch hung. Hay asserted that he was robbed of a gold chain and a stone seal that belonged to his watch and that Holland then attempted to rob him of the money in his pocket. During the scuffle, James Cunningham called out 'murder'.

Hay replied, 'Hold by your man, I have got one rascal secured. I hope you will secure the other.' After this exchange, Hay revealed that he saw a man running across the park. He then heard the sound of a horse's hooves nearby and called out for assistance, saying, 'Here is a man who has both attempted to rob and murder me.' Mr James Hay and Mr William Simpson then arrived and seized the robber, tying him up and placing him upon a cart to take to Haddington.

The court heard that Mr Hay formally identified James Holland as his attacker and that, during the robbery, he was dressed in coloured clothes from military stock. In their altercation, he repeatedly heard the accused use the term 'by Jesus', which led Hay to conclude that he was an Irishman. Following the apprehension of James Holland, Hay asked him if he had a pistol on him to carry out his threats. Holland replied, 'I only have a stick.' The remainder of the Crown's case involved Mr Hay's fellow travellers, who corroborated his evidence. As the prosecution ended, Lord Justice Clark commended the victim for 'the manly spirit he had displayed in resisting the daring attack'.

When James Wilson began the defence, limited avenues were available to refute the case put before them. Throughout the court proceedings, the defendant James Holland maintained that he had no accomplice with him on the night in question and that he was highly intoxicated and thus entirely ignorant of what had taken place until he found himself tied up on the cart. He maintained that the cloak he was wearing belonged to his wife and that he had taken it away merely in jest. Closing defence testimony followed from two highly respectable witnesses, officers in the Inniskilling Dragoons, who confirmed that James Holland was a diligent soldier known for an excellent character and 'sobriety, steadiness and attention'. A certificate from the

Commanding Officer of the regiment also attested to this.

At the end of the court case, Lord Justice Clerk, in his summing up, asserted to the jury that the case represented an 'excellent charge' and requested that they should give their verdict the following day, after the rising of the Court of Session. At two o'clock on Tuesday 13th December 1808, the jury returned their verdict as instructed, finding James Holland not guilty of the robbery by means of a plurality of voices. However, the jury did return a guilty verdict of felonious assault. James Holland was sentenced to transportation beyond the seas for life.

As a footpad thief, Holland would have been viewed by Georgian society as a man prone to violence, with antecedent behaviour. His was a sinful life of vice and crime. Although he was a military man, he was considered to have swapped this honest living and decided to commit robberies to fund his anti-social habits of drinking, gambling and prostitution. No consideration was given to the motivation behind Holland's actions – it is possible that he turned to a life of crime for the reasons already set out or that underlying causes involving poverty or unemployment contributed to his actions.

In the first decade of the 19th century, more than 200 types of crime could lead to execution, ranging from shoplifting to murder. While Holland's sentence was punitive, the outcome could have been far worse – if the robbery charge had been proven, this would have justified a capital sentence. It must be remembered that the judicial system of the early 18th century was acutely aware of how newspapers reported court cases, and stringent sentences acted as a quick deterrent to future perpetrators and reassured the middle-class readership that the rule of law was being applied judiciously.

Chapter 7

1819: The Fatal Effects of Intemperance

When the murder trial of Peter Bowers (19), a millwright from Haddington, got underway in Edinburgh on Monday 14th June 1819, it reached the High Court of Justiciary in a somewhat ambivalent manner. On 15th April 1819, the indictment specified that Bowers had murdered John Sandilands (66), a farm servant to the Earl of Dalhousie, by inflicting a fatal blow to his head. As the trial unfolded, it emerged that the altercation took place on the main road from Haddington to Colstoun House, famed as the oldest continuously inhabited home in Scotland – the Broun family can account for some 900 years of uninterrupted history.

Among the first witnesses to appear for the Crown was quarryman Alexander Napier. He confirmed to the Solicitor General J.A. Maconochie that he had seen Alexander Watt, Henry Phillips and John Sandilands drinking at Colstoun Toll House on his return from work at Bolton Quarry. The men came outside, and Watt and Phillips commenced leaping on the road. Some time later, a highly intoxicated Peter Bowers and his employer's son, Richard Catleugh, approached and challenged the men to a jumping competition for a two-pence wager. Bowers lost but refused to pay, and threatened to strike Alexander Watt with his axe – however, he was disarmed before doing so.

Such actions are associated with the Georgian era, which witnessed a 'golden age' of gambling. This was not merely the domain of the rich gentleman – many working-class men indulged in wagers which involved money that they could not afford to lose. Wagers were not confined to traditional gaming pursuits such as horse racing or playing cards. Particular favourites included betting on a range of events, from the gender of a baby about to be born to possible deaths during inclement weather or even simple jumping competitions.

After events calmed down, Napier indicated that Bowers' axe was returned to his possession as he intimated that he wished to travel home. The witness could not attest to hearing an exchange of words between Bowers and John Sandilands as the accused departed, but the next thing he saw was Bowers taking the blunt edge of his axe and striking at Sandilands' head. The axe incident was further corroborated by the medical evidence supplied by Mr Thomson, a surgeon from Haddington who attended to the victim. He asserted that Mr Sandilands had suffered a fatal wound to his left temple, which was several inches long and corresponded to the blunt edge of Bowers' axe.

Napier's testimony was given further credence by the next witness to appear before the justiciary – Alexander Watt, a farm servant on the Earl of Menstrie's estate – stipulated that an angry verbal exchange occurred between Sandilands and Bowers at some point earlier in the evening. The discourse concluded with John Sandilands stating to Bowers that, despite his advancing age, he would fight him. At the time of the attack, Watt indicated that John Sandilands was leaning against a tree outside the toll house. As Bowers passed him, yet another heated conversation took place between the two men. Bowers then attacked Sandilands, wielding his axe and striking the victim a single blow to the head. Neither Richard Catleugh nor Henry Phillips ventured any critical information in their Crown testimony except to state that both Bowers and Sandilands were very drunk on the evening in question.

Mr Richard Hay, Deputy Sheriff Clerk for Haddington, then elaborated on his dealings with the prisoner. The sheriff had declined to interview Bowers when he first appeared before him on the night of the murder as the prisoner was dazed and confused, suffering the effects of intoxication. Bowers' declaration was offered as evidence the following day, when details were set out of the prisoner's consumption of many alcoholic drinks at several different hostelries in the Gifford area on the day of the murder. The accused also confirmed that a disturbance had taken place at Colstoun Toll House but that he could not provide any further information.

The exculpatory evidence that followed refocused on the testimony of Richard Catleugh, who outlined that he, his father and Bowers had been engaged for just over a week on wheelwright work for Mr Trail of Gifford. On the day of the incident, the three men had enjoyed some alcoholic libations during the working day, and they were in good humour. Catleugh could not account for their overall alcohol intake but commented that it had been a warm day. They had dined at one o'clock in the afternoon and took no other refreshment until they left work at five o'clock.

Mr Trail, a bleacher from Gifford, admitted under examination by the defence that he supplied the three men with some spirits when they completed their job. The witness believed that the accused had taken about a glass and a half of strong denominated small spirits. Helen Wright, the landlady who had provided lodgings for Bowers, reported that he had not taken any alcohol during his time in her household, and demonstrated no unruly behaviour.

Richard Catleugh, a senior millwright, attested to the character of the accused, stating that Bowers had been in his employment for 13 months and had proven to be a hardworking, peaceable man with a good character. Previous employers, including John Eddington and William Wood, also took to the witness stand to deliver similarly glowing accounts of Bowers as sober, diligent and industrious. To conclude, the Solicitor General addressed the jury and stated that the facts of the case had been proven and supported by evidence. He added that 'murder was a crime that came home to the feelings of all men. Neither in morals nor law was intoxication considered as an extenuation of crime.' Accordingly, the prisoner's actions left the jury with no choice but to find him guilty as charged.

In his closing arguments, the defence counsel Mr Mungo Brown stipulated that his client's actions represented the folly of a young man rather than those of a habitual drunkard. In the event of a guilty verdict, Brown implored the jury to recommend that the Crown should show the accused mercy, but he earnestly encouraged them to return a verdict of culpable homicide. The jury then retired to consider their verdict. In less than 90 minutes, their Chancellor, Sir R.K. Dick, declared that the accused was guilty through a plurality of voices, but the jury unanimously and earnestly recommended mercy.

In giving his judgement, Lord Hermand asked, 'is a man, after committing one crime, to plead another in justification?' He then turned to the guilty man and exhorted him, 'To employ [your] time better than in vain expectations and [to] prepare [your]self for the awful fate that awaits [you]." Lord

Succoth wholeheartedly agreed with his colleague and designated the outcome 'an important verdict for the country's law'. The Lord Justice Clerk then passed sentence on the guilty man. On Wednesday 21st July, between eight o'clock and ten o'clock in the morning, the prisoner was to be executed, and his body given to professor of anatomy Dr Monroe for dissection.

Despite this capital punishment sentence, the court took less than three months to reverse their original decision and commute the death warrant to transportation for life. The court's leniency resulted in no small measure to the prisoner's attitude – he conducted himself with great patience and mildness.

Peter Bowers was one of 190 convicts transported aboard the ship *Mangles* on 29th March 1820. On arriving in New South Wales, Bowers was enacted to a contractor for seven years. He worked as a labourer and carpenter in Liverpool, Greater Sydney, until he was released from servitude in November 1828. Less than a year later, he married Sarah Wantling – a union that would produce two daughters. Peter Bowers lived for another 50 years and passed away in Armidale, New South Wales, in 1879.

Chapter 8

1829: The Vindictive Hawker

In the early 19th century, a small community named Abbey was located about one mile east of Haddington on the north bank of the River Tyne, consisting of several two-storey houses and a working mill. This sleepy backwater had an illustrious past, and, as its eponymous name suggests, an abbey dedicated to St Mary was founded on the site in 1178 by the Countess of Northumberland, Ada de Warenne. The Scottish Parliament also convened within the abbey walls on 7th July 1548, when agreement was reached that Mary, Queen of Scots, would be educated in France. This decision was in preparation for Mary's marriage to the French Dauphin – a union set out under the Treaty of Haddington.

Despite an auspicious heritage, the small burial ground where mother and daughter Catherine and Magdalene Franks are interred perhaps offers up the most compelling narrative in the long history of this small settlement. The crime of murder perpetrated against these women at the hands of Robert Emond nearly 200 years ago has echoed down the generations, and its savagery is as unsettling now as it was then.

The year 1829 proved to be a time of deep sorrow for Mrs Franks, seeing her widowed and left with two young daughters. Fortunately, her late husband was a valued member of Lord Elcho's staff and was thus granted a pension on his retirement, enabling his widow to retain her independence. As a result, Mrs Franks and her eldest daughter Magdalene resided in a small house at the outer boundary of Abbey, while her younger child, Catherine, lived with her sister and brother-in-law in North Berwick. This arrangement reduced her financial expenses and enabled her sister, without children of her own, to welcome a young person into her household.

On Wednesday 28th October 1829, a concerned neighbour, Mrs Dudgeon, asked James Storrie, a worker from the mill, to call on Mrs Franks. Mrs Dudgeon had become alarmed by her neighbour's squealing sow pig. Storrie approached the property, which was enclosed on three sides by a wall and bounded on the fourth by the mill's watercourse. Unable to gain access via the garden gate, Storrie climbed over the wall and found Mrs Franks dead in the pigsty with a deep wound to her throat. He quickly raised the alarm and returned with Mrs Dudgeon's husband, Alexander Dudgeon. Fearing for Magdalene's safety, the men entered the house, where they discovered her dead body on the bedroom floor.

When Superintendent John Lloyd entered the pigsty some time later, the seasoned Haddington constabulary officer was shocked by the savagery of the murder that had taken place. After completing his preliminary examination, Lloyd confirmed that Mrs Frank's watch, rings and earrings were missing. In the house, the Superintendent came upon the lifeless body of young Magdalene Franks and a ransacked chest of drawers, in which a secret compartment had been opened. Magdalene had received repeated blows to her skull, and on the floor beside her was a discarded knife and the footprint of a bloodied hobnail boot.

As was the standard practice of the day, the nearest living male relative, Mrs Frank's brother-in-law and Magdalene's uncle, was asked to identify their bodies. The gentleman in question, Mr Robert Emond, behaved very oddly during his brief conversation with Superintendent Lloyd and only reluctantly agreed to acquiesce to the formal request. Later that evening, the police were instructed to arrest Emond, who was found at the home of the deceased, where he had returned with a carpenter to measure the bodies for their coffins. Superintendent Lloyd informed Emond that he was now under arrest for murder, to which he replied, "Who could say that?"

Robert Emond was born in 1795 in the Scottish Borders market town of Selkirk; the youngest of four children. He had no apprentice trade and opted at the age of 14 to enlist in the 72nd Regiment in November 1809. During his eight years of military service, he was stationed in Ireland, proving unpopular with his contemporaries and officers. Upon receiving an honourable discharge from the army in March 1817, Emond began working as a travelling pedlar and, within two years, had gained enough capital to take out a hawker's[4] licence in Edinburgh.

Gaining some success in the trade, he acquired an English travelling salesman's licence in August 1822, which saw him travel throughout Northumberland. As Emond began to prosper, he purchased a horse and cart, which allowed him to carry a more varied assortment of goods to

---

[4] Hawker: A person who travels around selling goods, typically advertising them by shouting.

sell and expand his commercial enterprises. However, to improve his profits, Emond endeavoured unsuccessfully to defraud his creditors by concealing a large portion of his merchandise and presenting himself as having suffered heavy losses.

During his time as a travelling salesman, Emond became acquainted with his future wife, Magdalene, who grew up on the Duke of Gordon's estate. They married in 1827 and relocated to Sunderland. This move proved a difficult transition – Emond could not settle in the area. He professed a deep resentment of the local people, and his antecedence led the newly married couple to move their business to North Berwick, where they finally settled. However, their union proved less than successful as Mrs Emond was a hard worker with her own business while her husband was lackadaisical and prone to wandering off for large parts of the day. Emond's behaviour precipitated severe arguments between them and reciprocal blows during particularly heated exchanges. Emond's state of mind might even have been impaired as there was a history of mental illness in his family.

When Robert Edmond entered the dock, the public interest in his case was comparable to that in the infamous murder trial of William Burke,[5] who became a cause célèbre.

---

[5] Burke and Hare carried out a serious of 16 murders in Edinburgh over a ten-month period in 1828 and sold the bodies to Robert Knox for dissection in his anatomy classes. On their arrest Hare turned King's evidence which granted him immunity from prosecution. Burke was found guilty and sentenced to hang and his corpse was dissected and his skeleton is still displayed at the Anatomical Museum of Edinburgh Medical School. The case led to renewed moves in parliament to end the illicit trade of bodysnatching. The Anatomy Act in 1832, simultaneously ended the post-mortem punishment of dissection for murder and created a new stream of bodies for surgeons, who could now use bodies of the unclaimed workhouse poor.

Crowds clamoured to gain access to the courtroom, which meant that the main doors had to be barricaded. Those directly involved with the trial had to gain admittance via a ticket system at the Signet Library. Many within the public gallery commented that Robert Emond looked composed in the dock, and his image was not regarded as characteristic with that of a murderer. The accused was diminutive in height, at only five feet four inches in his bare feet, and had a thin, pallid countenance hidden under sandy coloured whiskers. Despite Emond's unassuming appearance, Guy Logan, in his 1928 exposition *Dramas of the Dock: True Stories of Crime*, characterises him as a surly man, 'given to brooding over real or fancied wrongs, which, in his warped mind, became intolerable injuries'.

When he appeared before Lord Gillies on Monday 8th February 1830 at the Court of Justiciary in Edinburgh, the indictment declared that Robert Emond (35), draper and grocer, formerly domiciled in North Berwick, on the night of 25th October 1829 or early the following morning murdered Mrs Catherine Franks (widow) (50) and her daughter Magdalene Franks (14) at their home in the hamlet of Abbey, near Haddington. The accused entered a plea of not guilty, and a declaration was made that no witnesses would appear for the defendant. The defence counsel would re-examine the Crown witnesses if necessary.

Mrs Marion Inglis took to the witness stand and, under oath, confirmed that she knew Mrs Franks and her daughter very well. She recounted the dead woman's daily routine and alluded to the fractious relationship she shared with her brother-in-law, Richard Emond. The witness believed that the mother and daughter had travelled to North Berwick to visit family at the time of the tragedy as no activity had been apparent at their house for several days.

Early on Wednesday morning, shouts of alarms roused Mrs Inglis from her bed. On approaching the Franks' house, she found her daughter and neighbour Margaret Anderson helping to carry the lifeless body of Mrs Franks out of the pigsty and into the family home. Mrs Inglis further explained to the court that, earlier in the year, a heated disagreement had erupted between the widowed Mrs Franks and her brother-in-law. The argument concerned some boxes of household linen and clothes forwarded to North Berwick ahead of Mrs Frank's intended visit. On arrival, Mrs Franks discovered that Emond had opened the items, which led to a full-blown argument between them.

Superintendent Lloyd subsequently took to the witness box and stated that an examination of Emond's home was carried out in the presence of the Sheriff Officer and General Dalrymple. A pair of boots was recovered, the imprints of which corresponded to the bloody footprints at the murder scene. Emond's clothes from the evening of the murders were found with blood on the shirt sleeves and in the trouser pockets. After this discovery, the prisoner was interviewed at Haddington Jail. In the course of the conversation, Emond declared 'that he deserved the gallows'. When Lloyd quizzed him on this statement, Emond replied that 'it was for the bad treatment he had given to his wife'.

As the trial moved on to consider the medical evidence, Mr Howden, the surgeon who carried out the post-mortem examinations, gave his findings. He concluded that Mrs Frank's throat had been cut, splitting her windpipe, gullet and carotid artery, and there were ten separate injuries to her head. Magdalene Franks suffered a significant injury to her cranium, inflicted by a heavy cutting instrument as the perpetrator beat her to death. The young girl's skull had been fractured several times, with eight different injuries apparent.

Death was ascertained to have had taken place two to three days before the discovery of the bodies, either late on the evening of 24th October or early the following morning. Mr Howden was shown articles of clothing belonging to the victims and the accused but could not offer an incontrovertible opinion on all the bloodstains.

The surviving child of Mrs Franks, Catherine (11), confirmed that she had attended church on the Sunday morning before her mother's death. On returning home, she found her aunt with a blistered mouth and torn wet clothes after her uncle had attempted to throw her down the garden well. She was saved from death at the last minute by a concerned neighbour. These alarming circumstances resulted from her aunt's refusal to supply money for her husband's new business venture. Fearing for their safety, Catherine and her aunt shared the same bedchamber that night, behind a bolted door.

On the following morning, Catherine revealed that the accused was absent from the family home, and, on his return, wore a dark coat. She reported that his trousers began to smoke as he approached the open fire, as if they were wet. She recounted to the court that her mother and Emond were on bad terms and had exchanged angry words during their last conversation.

The other witnesses included Mr Thomas Cron, who confirmed that he had seen Emond about a mile from Dirleton, travelling towards North Berwick, on the morning in question and had noted his dishevelled condition. Alison Webster described Emond's visit to her shop in Dirleton, some two miles from North Berwick – she was taken aback by Emond's appearance, noting that he was 'all blood about the mouth, both above and below'.

John Dunbar informed the court that he had known the accused for several years. He attested to the fact that Emond had, on several occasions, declared that there would 'never be peace for him and his wife while she corresponded with her sister'. Dunbar encountered Emond on the morning of Tuesday 28th October 1829, finding him in a sad state.

When Dunbar asked what was wrong, Emond replied that the devil had been busy with him. Further testimony came from Mr Dods, the Provost of Haddington, who decided to visit Emond in prison on receipt of correspondence from him. The prosecuting counsel asked Mr Dods if any information had emerged during the precognition[6] against Emond. The witness advised the court that Emond said that he did not see how they could find evidence to convict him.

Utilising witness testimony that outlined the defendant's dishevelled appearance and blood about his person, the prosecution counsel offered the jury a glimpse into his actions in the aftermath of the murders. Emond killed his sister-in-law Catherine Franks in revenge for what he saw as her continued interference in his married life. For Magdalene, her young life ended for no other reason than that she was a witness to her mother's death.

Lord Gillies then addressed the court, informing them that he would introduce two new witness testimonies from individuals who had been in prison alongside the accused. The judge detailed the objection put forward against this practice by the defence counsel but reiterated that the witnesses would be eligible for a King's Pardon despite not

---

[6] Precognition in Scots Law is the practice of both prosecution and defence taking a factual statement from witnesses after indictment or claim but before trial.

having faced trial for their alleged crimes. Robert Tait, recently released from Glasgow Jail, was the first to take the stand.

He revealed that he was formerly employed as a salesman in the warehouse of Inglis & Co., silk makers in Glasgow, and was arrested on a charge of theft. On 21st November 1829, he was brought to Edinburgh and put into ward No. 5 of the jail on Calton Hill. At his behest, Emond was allowed to sleep in this cell after 29th November. Tait stated that Emond did not sleep soundly, often waking up during the night shouting, 'Oh, that wretched passion'. His behaviour appeared to be that of a man in torment.

Over the next few days, Emond recounted the story of his life. When asked if he had carried out the murders, he replied, 'Oh yes, but do not speak of it. The very thought goes to my heart like a knife.' He insisted that all that he remembered was being in his sister-in-law's house and exchanging words with her, and then the deed was done, and indicated that he was surprised to hear from the constabulary that Magdalene was dead, as he had no recollection of killing her.

Under cross-examination from the defence, Robert Tait clarified that Emond visited his sister-in-law on Sunday evening and blamed his actions towards her for not taking the sacrament that day. Lord Gillies interceded at this point of the interview and noted that the information put forth by the witness had been obtained over several conversations with Emond. Under oath, the second witness, Daniel Murray, confirmed that he was a clerk in Glasgow and had been charged with theft alongside Tait. Murray described the accused as very restless and uneasy in his manner. Although Murray did not ask to hear details of the murders, the accused introduced the subject in conversation with him.

After giving this testimony, the defendant put forward a declaration stating that he had mistreated his wife on the day in question and taken her to the well, but he reiterated that he had no intention of throwing her into it. On the night they argued, his wife had told him to go away, and he had left the house and roamed among the fields, unaware of where he was going. He returned home to North Berwick the following day and, later in the week, was informed of the murder of Mrs Franks and her daughter, with whom he claimed he had remained on good terms.

Lord Gillies then addressed the jury and indicated that the murders had been premediated in nature, stating that, regardless of the emotional duress the accused was under, he had the foresight to take Mrs Franks' wedding ring and earrings and therefore suggesting that the motive of the crime was robbery. Lord Gillies also noted that Emond had possessed the state of mind to dispose of the murder weapon.

The Lord Advocate declared the murders 'hideous in their atrocity' – particularly the unnecessary and purposeless killing of the young girl. He reiterated that this was a case of great importance, and, from the evidence put forward by the Crown, he felt that a verdict of guilty was warranted. The judge asked whether Emond had anything to add to his defence to avoid the death penalty. The accused noted that he was innocent of intention: 'I had not thought of killing Mrs Franks when I left my room that morning, still less of injuring my niece.'

The jury took less than 30 minutes to return a guilty declaration, which was met with shouts of approval. Emond was sentenced to hang on Wednesday 17th March 1830. Afterwards his body was to be transferred to the medical department of Edinburgh University and used for public dissection. In the weeks that followed, Emond came face to face with his wife in an exchange that gave neither comfort nor resolution.

Mrs Emond was prevailed upon to shake hands with her husband, but, when he grasped her hand, she experienced an involuntary shudder and was heard to say, 'Oh that hand, that hand!' It is possible that a plan was thwarted in which Emond's sister intended to supply him with oxalic acid to enable him to commit suicide. This was not to ease his passing or to avert his family's shame of a public execution. Instead, it was planned in the erroneous belief that, if Emond committed suicide, his belongings would not be forfeited to the Crown.

On the day before his hanging, Robert Emond was transferred by hackney coach from Calton Jail to the lock-up house. Reverend Porteous stayed with Emond, offering continual support, but the prisoner remained composed and tranquil. As the hour of his demise approached, he was asked how he felt. He replied, 'My mind is quite sound and as clear as ever. My grief does not affect the mind so much as the body. I hope God will give me the strength to go through it and perhaps speak too.'

At eight in the morning on Wednesday 17th March 1830, Baillies Anderson and Morton appeared and the procession got underway towards the place of execution at Liberton's Wynd.

Some minutes later, Robert Emond ascended the scaffold, and, as the crowd thronged with noise, awaiting the justice of the hangman, Emond's lasts words were a hushed whisper to the executioner, 'Let my sister Betty Emond in Selkirk know that I died in peace and that I justly merit death.' While the murderous exploits of Burke and Hare fitted well with Edinburgh's seedy and nefarious underbelly, the crimes perpetrated by Robert Emond were incongruous with Abbey's tranquil countryside setting.

Chapter 9

1877/1883: Murders at the Asylum

The Victorian mental asylum conjures up images of suffering and degradation, with inmates routinely restrained physically and left to the mercy of their keepers. However, by the second half of the 19th century, a conscious effort had emerged to develop a more humane and therapeutic environment to treat people with mental illness. Under the terms of the Scottish Lunacy Act, 1857, the General Board was established, which advanced an institutional approach towards mental illness formulated around the precept of work.

When the purpose-built Haddington District Asylum opened in 1866, it could accommodate 90 people and comprised a recreational hall, central administration area and kitchen. Wings flanked the property to accommodate the patients in single rooms and day rooms on the ground floor. As was the standard of the day, there were workshops for the male residents and laundry and washhouse facilities for the women.

Like many of its contemporary establishments, Haddington District Asylum was inspired by the Victorian country house estate, held up as an example of good living.

The institution was purposely situated in a rural location to address the practicalities of site planning and to avoid spatial constraints that had, in the past, led to overcrowding and squalid conditions. An element of financial shrewdness was also at play. These newly developed institutions could accommodate much larger numbers of patients in one site, representing a centralisation policy involving economies of scale by no longer utilising smaller cost-prohibitive establishments.

Many people in 19th-century British society viewed mental illness as a blight on the nation and relocating such patients to rural establishments was almost an attempt to hide a guilty secret. Nonetheless, institutions such as Haddington Asylum were well conceived, generously funded, adequately staffed and made no effort to hide their location or objective.

However, during this era, a genuine worry existed within the medical community that overcrowding and increasing numbers of the public presenting with mental health issues could overwhelm the system. In retrospect, the increased number of cases presented can be attributed to the establishment of new infrastructure throughout Scotland which addressed a previous lack of institutional provision. Asylum admissions were also heavily influenced by the 1875 'lunacy grant' – a government stipend provided to local authorities as a fiscal incentive to improve provisions for lunacy.

Despite these good intentions, the reality was that institutions such as Haddington Asylum were home to men and women suffering from poorly understood conditions. Irrespective of new clinical approaches to mental illness, which included physical examination, case note recording and the confinement of new patients to bed, there remained a subjective diagnosis policy, while clinicians lacked the modern spectrum of treatments that we now take for granted.

Doctors and commissioners of such establishments openly promoted a policy of non-restraint through the removal of the prison-like aspects of asylum accommodation. While this was an audacious strategy that was applauded by Victorian reformers of the day, it failed to consider the risk of potential violence and threats to patients and staff members alike. Hindsight and advances in medical practices enable arbitrary judgements to be made but the question remains whether events at Haddington Asylum had an unfortunate air of inevitability to them.

On Wednesday 10th January 1877, as the country slowly turned its mind to Queen Victoria's ruby anniversary, a gruesome attack occurred at Haddington Asylum. As was the institution's daily routine, at nine o'clock in the morning, patients John Edington and Robert Fortune were escorted by a staff member to the shoe workshop, an annex building where they changed their footwear in preparation for working outside in the asylum grounds. In the briefest of moments while the attendant was absent from the workshop, Fortune attacked Edington with a hedge knife. Such was the ferocity of the single blow that Edington's skull was fractured, inducing a laceration of the brain and instantaneous death. When the murder was discovered, the perpetrator appeared calm and subdued, watching his victim's lifeless body.

Robert Fortune (30), who originated from Gifford, had arrived in Haddington Asylum some two and a half years previously from Edinburgh's Morningside Asylum with a reputation as a dangerous lunatic. However, the former Scots Greys soldier never displayed any violent propensities during his time at Haddington and was known to work peacefully in the company of other patients. In comparison, the victim, John Edington (41), was a former farm servant and native of

Whitekirk, who had resided at the asylum for over ten years, demonstrating that he was a docile and largely trustworthy patient.

On Monday 5th February 1877, Robert Fortune appeared before the Lord Justice Clerk Baron Moncrieff at the High Court of Justiciary in Edinburgh charged with the murder of John Edington. As the case got underway, the defence counsel Mr Campion called Dr Thomas Howden, a medical attendant from Haddington Asylum, to the witness box to attest to the perpetrator's state of mind. Dr Howden stated that the patient Robert Fortune was a 'confirmed lunatic'. Solicitor General John MacDonald pressed Dr Howden to expand on his statement and provide further details to the court.

In Dr Howden's view, Fortune could not comprehend the charge of murder against him. He could not provide any rational instructions to his defence counsel, and any testimony put forward during the proceedings could not be relied upon because of his poor mental condition. The Lord Justice Clerk interceded at this juncture, stating that the prisoner had attributed the murder of John Edington to the Holy Ghost. On other occasions, when quizzed about the crime, he refused to say anything about it, remaining sullen and reserved. Dr Arthur Mitchell, a Commissioner of the General Board of Lunacy, concurred with the earlier medical testimony after conducting his own examination of the prisoner, classifying Robert Fortune as insane.

That a dispute took place between the murderer and his victim was not verified – indeed, they had peaceably coexisted during their time at Haddington Asylum. With legal and medical consensus, the case against Robert Fortune was classified as 'pro loco et tempore', translated as 'without place and time'. In Scottish legal terms, this prevented the indictment from proceeding as the facts could not be fully determined. The prisoner was consequently removed from the asylum environment because of the physical threat he posed and was remanded to Perth Prison.

Less than six years later, another murder at Haddington Asylum, on 6th September 1883, shared many similarities with its predecessor. At around 5.30pm on Thursday afternoon, Andrew Buchanan (30), a native of Prestonpans, attacked Robert Darg White (29), a former Haddington bank clerk who had resided at the asylum for over six years. On the day of the murder, both patients were asserted to have left the day room, where they had been under the charge of warden Alexander Horne, and entered the adjacent lavatory. They had only just gone into the room when Buchanan seized White by the throat and threw him to the floor.

While his victim was lying prone on the ground, Buchanan kneeled on his chest and brutally and mercilessly hammered the unfortunate man's face and head with his clenched right fist. Fellow patient Robert Lawrie witnessed the murderous events and quickly sought help from the warden, who called the governor, Mr Mowat. Robert White's facial features were unrecognisable because of his injuries and, by the time Dr Ronaldson arrived, he had died.

When the murder case reached the High Court of Justiciary on Monday 5th November 1883, defence counsel Mr Napier cited the mental fragility of the accused and argued that he was not fit to make a plea at a murder trial. In the medical evidence, Mr James Bruce Ronaldson, representing Haddington Asylum, stated that, on 3rd August 1883, Andrew Buchanan was brought into the institution suffering from an acute mania and that, in his considered medical opinion, the prisoner was psychotic.

Additional expert medical opinion was supplied by Dr James A. Sidey, the famous clinician and son of the distinguished Edinburgh surgeon Charles Sidey. James Sidey concurred that Andrew Buchanan was insane and unfit to stand trial. Prosecution counsel represented by Mr Brand did not dispute the evidence set out before the court and made no further declaration on behalf of the Crown. As in the previous case, Lord Young gave the usual order that the prisoner should be imprisoned at her Majesty's pleasure.

As murderers unfit to stand trial, Robert Fortune and Andrew Buchanan became known as prisoner-patients. In line with the judicial system of the late 19th century, they were remanded to the criminal lunatic department of Perth Prison – the Scottish equivalent of Broadmoor. Despite a more enlightened ethos in treating such individuals, protection of members of the public was prioritised over individual rights.

In the 21st century, it is exceedingly difficult for most people to articulate what life was like for prisoner-patients, but J. Bruce Thomson, a resident surgeon from Perth Prison during this period, provides a window into daily life for such men. Fortune and Buchanan fit into what was called a 'homicidal class', a salient feature of which was the transitory character of their insanity. As Thomson notes, 'The impulse to homicide seizes the patient suddenly, and as suddenly passes away.'

The prison asylum 'endeavoured to keep pace with evolving treatment methods and provided increased care and attention to all criminal lunatics of the day'. After periods of incarceration at Perth Prison, both Robert Fortune and Andrew Buchanan returned to Haddington Asylum, where they died in 1900 and 1915, respectively. Ultimately, Perth Prison adhered to the Victorian maxim of protecting the public from those suffering from mental illness, yet it also protected prisoner-patients from Victorian prejudices.

Chapter 10

1902: St Germains

The picturesque mansion house of St Germains is situated in Tranent, adjacent to Seton Castle. At the turn of the 20th century, the estate adjoined the main North British Railway line to the south at a midway point between the villages of Cockenzie and Longniddry. The estate comprised some 1,100 acres, and the grounds were home to an undulating topography of manicured lawns, magnificent elms and walnut trees with a long driveway that stretched from the gatehouse to the main house.

Nestled to the east are ancient ruins, believed to have once been a medieval hospital dedicated to the Star of Bethlehem Order. Founded by the de Quincy family for the Knights Hospitallers, the site can be accurately assigned to circa 1170–1180 and Robert de Quincy. In the Ragman Rolls,[7] reference is made to 'Bartholomew Mestre de la Maison de St Germen, anno 1296'. This referred to St

---

[7] **Ragman Rolls** refer to the collection of instruments with which Scotland's nobility and gentry gave allegiance to King Edward I of England between May 1291 and the final award in favour of Balliol in November 1292 and again in 1296.

Germanus of Auxerre, known as the Battling Bishop, who, in the 5th century, visited Britain to increase support for the Catholic Church and the teaching of divine grace, countering the teaching of Pelagius. Germanus was a soldier in his earlier life and was involved in the defeat of Saxons and Picts, extolling his troops to fight with the battle cry 'Alleluia'.

The moniker of St Germains remained synonymous with Scotland. In the 17th century, it became associated with the exiled Jacobite court. In 1689 James VII and his Queen, Mary of Modena, fled to France after being deposed in the wake of the Glorious Revolution the previous year. As a sign of support, Louis XIV of France put the castle of Saint-Germainen-Laye, near Versailles, at the disposal of James VII, enabling him to maintain a Royal Court and attract, reward and encourage those sympathetic to the Jacobite cause.

In contrast, the estate of St Germains enjoyed a more settled existence as the Seton family, who were also senior members of the Templar organisation in Scotland, acquired the lands via marriage to the De Quincy heiress. Despite most of the revenues from St Germains being gifted by James IV to King's College, Aberdeen, in 1494, the Seton family continued to be custodians of the estate until it was forfeited after the Jacobite uprising of 1715. In 1782 David Anderson purchased St Germains and dramatically enhanced the mid-18th century mansion with a seven bayfront range – a fitting extension to a property that would act as his family's residence for the next century.

Accordingly, the arrival of Mr and Mrs John Brooks in the parish of Tranent in 1901 could not help but pique the interest of polite society. After all, the married couple had just taken out a ten-year lease on the St Germains estate from its millionaire owner, Mr Tennent of Wellpark Brewery, Glasgow. Little did the gentlefolk of the county realise, however, that within a year that same couple would become synonymous with a murder-suicide tragedy at this historic residence.

John Brooks was a man of independent financial means. He was born in 1850 at Crawshaw Hall near the village of Crawshawbooth, nestled at the edge of the Pennine Hills just north of the market town of Rawtenstall in Lancashire. His grandfather was a significant quarry owner in the area, responsible for building the entire mineral tramway network that linked multiple quarries in Lancashire. Equally important to John was his Uncle Thomas, the Rt Hon. Lord Crawshaw (1st Baron), the High Sheriff of Lancashire and founding member of the Rossendale hunt.

In 1874 in Tangier John Brooks married Louisa Annette Edla Drummond Hay, the daughter of Sir John Drummond Hay, a man of singular gifts. During his tenure as a mere attaché, he succeeded his chief as British Consul General to the Court of Morocco in 1844, thus beginning a career that lasted for more than 40 years. Such was the importance of Sir John's career in international diplomacy. Louisa would, in later life, co-author a biography about her father.

The marriage produced one son, John Hay Brooks, who, in adulthood entered a career in the South of Scotland Militia Artillery, rising to the rank of Captain and in the days before the tragedy, he was billeted with his regiment in Dunbar. He also gained fame in later life for opening the Brooks family home in Tangier at 'Senya el Hashti' to the artist Henri Matisse, who utilised the beautiful Moroccan gardens to create three evocative landscapes, intended as a triptych.

At four o'clock in the morning on Monday 30th June 1902, St Germains was awoken by reports of gunfire. As the staff were acutely aware of Mr Brooks' recent indifferent health and his bouts of eccentricities, a state of alarm erupted throughout the house. On entering the room on the ground floor where the couple slept, the housemaid was horrified to find her worst fears realised. John Brooks was lying on the floor in a pool of blood, a discharged sporting rifle beside him, while Louisa Brooks' head was still resting on the blood-stained pillow. Although both were dead, the coachman was dispatched for medical assistance and informed Tranent's police authorities, some two miles away.

Dr Miller, who had been consulted by Mr Brooks the previous week, drove to St Germains immediately and was joined at the crime scene by Inspector Campbell, the chief detective from Tranent Constabulary. Dr Miller ascertained that Louisa Brooks, who had been confined to her room for some days by an attack of bronchitis, sustained two fatal gunshot wounds to the face at point-blank range while her husband died from a self-inflicted gunshot wound to the head.

During the early hours of the morning, Mr Brooks had woken and procured a gun from the adjacent gun room, loaded it and fired twice at his wife, before turning the weapon on himself. Later in the day, Superintendent Mann of Haddington and the Deputy Procurator Fiscal, Mr Stirling, arrived to follow up the initial investigations.

As news of the distressing events spread throughout Tranent, it emerged that, before relocating to St Germains, the Brooks family lived in Berwickshire, where they resided for some years at Oxendean Tower, near Duns. During their tenure at St Germains, the couple, both in their early fifties, regularly attended Rev. Caesar's sermon at Tranent Parish Church, although they were not well known in the village.

Mr Brooks was a tall man who carried himself with a military bearing, while his late wife was warm hearted and known to be involved with many charitable organisations. They travelled to their estate in Tangier in September 1901 and returned to St Germains less than a month before the double tragedy. During Mr Brooks' travels abroad, his health took a turn for the worse. Those who knew him noted the stark change in his appearance when he returned home. Although Mr Brooks' state of health made it necessary in previous years for him to winter abroad, there was no indication that his mind was in any way affected. The tropical climate in Tangier did not agree with Mr Brooks and, after seeking medical advice, he decided to return to Scotland immediately.

On returning to St Germains, Mr Brooks complained to his wife and family of recurring pains in his head and consulted Dr Miller, who advised that a consultant's services should be engaged to provide a diagnosis and options for treatment. The patient visited the eminent brain surgeon, Dr Byrom Bramwell of Edinburgh. Unfortunately, though, there was no time for medical intervention to improve Mr Brooks' condition, and nothing that could prevent the terrible events that were about to transpire.

As quickly as the police investigation was opened, the fiscal office concluded that it was a case of murder-suicide while John Brooks was of unsound mind. The reasoning behind John Brooks' actions can only be hinted at, but the apparent decline in his physical wellbeing and his chronic pain point to a degenerative neurological disease, especially when the services of Dr Byrom Bramwell were consulted. In conclusion, this tale added a macabre twist to the long history of St Germains, while the tragedy of Mr and Mrs Brooks ended for them when they were buried together on 3rd July

1902, side by side in the old burial ground at Tranent churchyard.

Chapter 11

1905: The Half Moon Plantation Child

Archerfield Estate is situated in the parish of Dirleton, around two miles west of the picturesque town of North Berwick, and hugs the dramatic coastline of East Lothian. Over its lifetime, Archerfield has boasted a list of residents from the Nisbet family, feudal barons of Dirleton through to the time of Prime Minister Herbert Asquith, whose brother-in-law owned the property. However, in 1905, a child's death at the Half Moon Plantation, within the grounds of the country estate, saw an unforeseen narrative unfold, fuelled by sympathy and horror.

On the afternoon of Tuesday 3rd January 1905, Hugh Kenny was engaged as ground beater at Archerfield, helping to raise game birds for the shoot, when he spotted a small brown paper package bound with twine lying under a privet bush. On inspection, the parcel was found to contain the body of a young child covered with a discoloured white robe. Mr Kenny quickly informed the head gamekeeper of the estate, who reported the matter to the police in the nearby village of Gullane.

Constable Harper was despatched to the scene of the incident and identified that the child's body was found close to the property's main carriageway, known as the 'Avenue', some 500 yards from the house. The location itself, known as Half Moon Plantation, consisted of fir trees and mixed forest and extended along the north side of the post road to the southern entrance of the lodge house. After the preliminary investigations were completed, the child's body was conveyed to the outhouse at Dirleton churchyard. Dr John Liddle Crombie from North Berwick examined the body and pronounced that the child was about one month old at the time of death, and had been dead for some five months. Crombie, assisted by his colleague Dr Ronaldson, carried out a post-mortem examination, but no cause of death was established.

Despite the sparse medical evidence, the authorities were quick to act. Within two days of the body being discovered, a young woman was arrested in Glasgow and a man in Edinburgh. The latter was charged with involvement in the child's death. The two accused were taken to Haddington Court, where they made their declarations before the Sheriff and were both subsequently committed to prison ahead of further legal proceedings. The Crown appointed the Solicitor General, Edward Salvesen K.C., and the advocate depute Mr Younger to prosecute, while Mr Smith Clark and Mr Hunter appeared for the defence.

When the case began before Lord McLaren on Monday 27th March, the courtroom was congested, with people from Haddington and the surrounding districts in attendance. The charge asserted that John Rose (33), a horse dealer normally resident at 9 Lennox Street Lane, Edinburgh and employed as a groom at the Archerfield Estate, had suffocated and murdered the illegitimate female child of Miss Jean Scott in the Half Moon Plantation on 22nd July 1904.

The first witness, Miss Jean Scott (22), stated that she had entered service at Archerfield as a second table maid on 18th May 1902 (Whitsunday). Since then, she had become friendly and eventually intimate with the accused. On 11th November of the following year, Jean took up a new position in Grosvenor Street, Edinburgh, where she discovered she was pregnant. At the beginning of 1904, Jean left Edinburgh for Newcastle to shield her condition from other people. On the preceding Friday, before leaving the city, she met Rose and told him about her pregnancy. He made no denial of this.

Throughout Jean's time in service at Bainbridge Hall, Newcastle, she tried to initiate correspondence with Rose, without success. On 4th May, she wrote: 'Dear John, I wonder if it will interest you to know that I am still alive. Why should we not be friends? I have given you little trouble.'

In her letters, she described the final few months of her pregnancy, stating, 'How hard it has been. No one knows what troubles I have gone through.' She remonstrated with Rose: 'You might have been kind enough to write as you promised. I cannot think why you did not. You are usually kind-hearted.' In a subsequent letter, she wrote, 'I want to make a bargain with you. If you give me 10 pounds or 12 pounds, you will never hear from me again. I have not enough money to carry me through, and I do not see why I should starve while you enjoy yourself', concluding that, 'I have given you a chance to keep things quiet, but if you do not, then I do not care who knows, and I will make you pay up to the last penny. I do not see why you should get off easy with everything.' She received no answer to that letter.

As the birth date neared, Jean intimated to the court that she entered the Maternity Hospital in Newcastle, where she gave birth to a healthy female child on 4th July 1904. After the birth, Jean negotiated a new job for herself and wrote to Rose once again. She advised him that she was travelling to Gullane on 22nd July and requested that he meet her at eight o'clock that evening. Jean left Newcastle early on that morning and journeyed with her baby to Edinburgh, then on to Gullane. Upon her arrival, she began walking towards Archerfield and met a wagon party en route to the estate driven by the accused, who failed to acknowledge her. On reaching Archerfield, Jean asserted to the court that she had asked the children of Mrs Nicholson, who kept the lodge house, whether the carriage had returned. Mrs Nicholson came forward and intimated that it had.

Jean then slowly walked along the avenue and waited for Rose under the tree canopy. He arrived some time later on a bicycle. In the heated exchange that followed, Jean asked Rose what support she could expect for their child, at which point he denied paternity and taunted her about her promiscuous relationships. At this juncture in their conversation, a man walked past, later identified by the accused as Mr Woodcock, the head gardener.

Rose eventually succumbed to Jean's demands and gave her 10 shillings in silver, promising to meet her on the Drem road the following day. Throughout their discussion, Jean held the baby in her arms and, when Rose became abusive, she threatened to inform his employer. In a fit of anger, she laid the child at Rose's feet and travelled back to Gullane, where she stayed the night.

When she met Rose the following morning, Jean asked where the child was, to which he replied, 'She is up in the wood with your handkerchief in her mouth.' Reminded that she was under oath, Jean stated that she wanted to look for her child, but the accused had prevented her from doing so. Rose made it clear that she would be blamed for the child's death and reiterated that she should leave. Jean took the train from Drem to Portobello and joined the tramcar for Edinburgh, subsequently travelling to Stirling to stay with her uncle.

In the following months, Jean corresponded sporadically with Christina Logan, a former colleague at Archerfield, and admitted that she was the woman who had been seen entering the estate with a child. Miss Logan was told that the child was safe and forwarded a remittance of one pound for the child's upkeep. Jean Scott admitted that she did not look back or return when she left her baby with Rose. When Rose informed her the following day that her handkerchief was in the child's mouth, she understood him to mean that he had suffocated the child, which she did not believe.

Under questioning, Rose advised the court that he believed that Jean Scott had been intimately involved with another man in the months leading up to her move to Newcastle. Rose further stated that at no point had Jean communicated to him that she had given birth to a baby. Lord McLaren interceded, stating to the jury, 'Miss Scott did not write telling Rose about the child, but she thought he would know from what she told him before she went away.'

Mrs Nicholson, lodge-keeper at Archerfield, corroborated Jean Scott's testimony to their brief conversation on the evening of the 22nd July in her evidence, indicating that she had seen the child in Scott's arms. However, under cross-examination from Mr Hunter, the witness admitted that she had not seen the baby's face, meaning that she may not have been alive. Margaret Peattie (13) of Marine Cottage, Archerfield, told the court that, on the evening in question, she passed Jean Scott carrying nothing other than an umbrella, which she pulled out in front of her when she saw Margaret, as if to hide her face.

Christina Logan was asked how she had come upon the information linking Rose to the child. Miss Logan replied that it was from nothing that she had personally seen and came rather from her knowledge of Rose's character. David White, a fellow groom from the estate, noted to the court that he had previously seen Scott and Rose together, although he stated that he had also seen Jean Scott with other men, for unknown reasons.

Richard Rae, custodian of the prison buildings in Haddington, stated that, while John Rose was in his custody, he advised him that he knew nothing of the matter at the Half Moon Plantation. Rose claimed that he only learned about the child's death when he received a letter from Jean Scott advising him of her actions. Mr Rae told the prisoner that it was regrettable that he did not have the letter to corroborate this, at which point Rose intimated to Rae that the letter might be found in his box at the stables in Edinburgh, a discovery which Detective Inspector McIntosh later attested to in court.

When Dr Crombie appeared before the court to give his medical testimony, he declared that it was impossible to tell the cause of the child's death. In his opinion, her heart and lungs were normal – however, after such a lapse of time, if suffocation had been the cause of death, the appearance of congestion would have gone.

The medical evidence for the defence was presented by Dr Joseph Bell, the inspiration behind Arthur Conan Doyle's Sherlock Holmes. Bell confirmed that, if the post-mortem report stated that the child's heart and lungs were normal, suffocation could not have been the cause of death. However, he concurred with his colleague Dr Crombie that he would not expect to find signs of suffocation after such a lapse of time, and he was also unable to identify a definitive cause of death.

As the case drew to a close, Lord McLaren, asked the jury to consider the discrepancies in the evidence, especially relating to whether the witness Jean Scott was carrying the child when she met the accused. If they thought that the charge had been proven, he indicated that he hoped that they would not shrink from their duty. If there was doubt, however, he instructed that it was right that the prisoner should have the benefit of acquittal, which the law allowed.

Jean Scott had occupied the witness box for the majority of the hearing and had to deal with a cross-examination that not only questioned her moral virtue but put forward a scenario of events that could have put her in the dock on a charge of infanticide. John Rose was portrayed by his counsel as one man among many, further blackening Jean Scott's character.

In the end, the jury returned to the court with their decision after less than ten minutes – a verdict of not guilty. As John Rose heard the decision, he was greeted with loud applause in the courtroom, and, as he left the court building and moved out into Parliament Square, he was met by a large crowd of well-wishers showing their hearty approval of the decision. As for Jean Scott, no charges were laid against her. As in so many tragedies involving children, culpability for the baby's death was never established.

Chapter 12

1907: The Golfer's Lament

Nearly every conceivable modern sport can trace its roots back to an earlier incarnation, and golf is no different. Some 2,000 years ago, the sport of *paganica* was played in the Roman Empire, while the reign of the Ming Dynasty (1368–1644) saw the game of *chuiwan* developed, involving 'hitting a ball with a stick while walking'. Add into the mix the Dutch game of *kolven* and the Belgian game of *chole,* and it is self-evident that the origins of golf lie in the ball and stick games of antiquity. Despite its diverse beginnings, the genesis of the modern game of golf can be traced directly to the shores of Scotland in the 15th century, when the vital missing ingredient was added – the hole.

Golf emerged from a game played on the east coast of Scotland, near Edinburgh, where a club or bent stick was used to hit a pebble around tracks or over sand dunes. Such was the popularity of the game that King James II of Scotland had to issue an edict banning it in 1457 as many soldiers were neglecting their military training in favour of golf, at a time when the country anticipated an English invasion. Not until some 45 years later was golf given the royal seal of approval, when King James IV of Scotland (1473–1513) became the self-styled first golfing monarch.

With such patronage, the popularity of golf spread throughout the royal houses of Europe, and Mary, Queen of Scots, introduced the game to France. Some 200 years later, golf finally achieved sporting status when The Honourable Company of Golfers (who played at Leith Links, Musselburgh Old Links and, eventually, Muirfield) drew up a set of rules in 1744, which still act as the basis of the game to this day, with several conventions adopted in their entirety by the Royal and Ancient Golf Club of St Andrews.

Just as Scotland can lay claim to being the home of golf, East Lothian can rightly state that it has also produced many virtuoso exponents of the sport. However, many of these notable personalities did not originate from the rich and landed families of the area. Instead, they emerged from working-class backgrounds and had full-time jobs, dedicating their meagre leisure time to improving their game. Among that select group of people was Henry 'Harry' Gullane, a native of North Berwick. He was born into a fishing family headed by James Gullane, who also worked as a part-time golf caddy, and his wife Janet, at 4 Market Place, North Berwick, on 19th May 1874.

Like many other golfers, Harry had worked hard to become a first-rate player, and, in April 1893, he earned his professional licence or 'ticket' at North Berwick's famous West Links course. Harry was duly appointed as the first professional at Gullane Golf Club and appeared in 1894 as a club representative to celebrate the opening of Luffness Golf Club. Less than two years later, Harry appeared in the Open Championship at Muirfield, further enhancing his reputation as a proponent of the sport. On the back of his continuing success, Harry decided to emigrate to America, travelling from Liverpool aboard the S.S. *Rhynland* and arriving in Philadelphia on 20th January 1897.

Quick to make an impression, Harry became the golf professional and greenkeeper at the Philadelphia Country Club – a testament to his golf skills and winning personality. At the beginning of 1898, Harry took part in a professional tournament at Lakewood, New York, and several challenge matches ensued in the following months. Most notably, Harry partnered Jamie Campbell against W.H. 'Bert' Way and Jack Harrison from the Meadowbrook Club, a private golf and hunting club based in Jericho, New York. The match consisted of two rounds of golf at Philadelphia and two at Meadowbrook, with a winning purse of 200 dollars.

In the end, the results of such matches were irrelevant – while the winner's fee was most welcome, a far more subtle dynamic was at work. The real importance of such competitions had two main functions. First, they were highly influential in generating publicity for players, both at domestic and international level. Second, they fired the imaginations of rival club members and brought new players to the game. Little did Harry Gullane realise, but this heralded a golden point in his professional golfing career.

The same year he partnered Jamie Campbell, Harry added his name to the history books, winning the first-ever professional tournament in the Philadelphia area. Participating as part of a select group of ten invited professionals, Gullane proved unstoppable at the Huntington Valley Country Club and won by some 12 strokes. This was a remarkable achievement given that the course was classed as unplayable and that Gullane's closest rival, the eventual runner-up, was one Willie Anderson, a fellow North Berwick man who would go on to win the US Open four times. Harry Gullane continued his winning ways when he shared first prize with Anderson at a tournament held at Baltusrol Golf Club, New Jersey, where Anderson was the club professional.

Harry's custom was to return home to North Berwick to spend the winter months with his family and friends. Buoyed by his success, though, he returned to the United States the following spring. The year 1899 demonstrated that Harry Gullane was more than just a talented golf professional as he displayed his solid head for business. He formed a mutually beneficial association with *Marshall E. Smith & Brothers*, a well-known and respected sporting goods store in Philadelphia, where he provided golf lessons and fitted customers for clubs.

In addition to this entrepreneurial sideline, Harry was appointed as the first golf professional to the St David's Club, Pennsylvania, where his skill as a course designer came to the fore. He supervised the expansion and completion of the club's new 18-hole course at Lancaster Pike. With this success under his belt, Harry went on to set out a nine-hole golf course at Pennsylvania's elegant West Chester Golf and Country Club, which opened in 1900. Harry Gullane played in several US Open tournaments and achieved his highest finishing position – a credible eighth – at the 1899 championship at the Baltimore Country Club, Maryland, where he won 25 dollars.

In 1901 Harry Gullane decided to return home to North Berwick permanently, and it is here that we enter the realms of conjecture to explore his motives for this move. Having travelled extensively in the United States, Harry had perhaps reached a point in his life where he craved a return to his family and the simpler times of his youth. By 1907 Harry Gullane had been back home in East Lothian for over five years, and his life had taken on a more sedate appearance. With his brother Andrew, he gave golfing lessons on North Berwick's West Links and he had recently married Margaret

Brown, a laundrymaid from a well-known local fisherman's family.

The couple set up home at 5 Law Road, North Berwick, and this should have been a happy time for the newlyweds. Unfortunately, though, the marriage was less than nine months old when, on Wednesday 1st May 1907, tragedy befell them. Just before midnight, Harry got out of bed, and an argument developed between him and his wife Margaret, resulting in him striking her a single blow with a hammer. In a state of panic, fearing that he had killed his wife, Harry quickly fled from the family home, dressed only in his bedclothes.

The following morning, masonry workers found a body in a mutilated condition in the Law Quarry. The body was identified as Harry Gullane (32). He was assumed to have taken his own life by jumping from North Berwick Law, a conical hill rising some 600 feet above sea level, known as the Grey Rock. Mr Gullane fell from a height of 70 feet and landed among rough stones, accounting for the deep cuts on his face and torso. Death would have been instantaneous.

Harry's widow survived her injury and lived another 26 years, dying in Edinburgh in 1933 at the age of 50. The events of that tragic and perplexing night were never fully established as Harry's actions were entirely out of character. Over 100 years after his death, he is known as one of the early Scottish golfing pioneers. In the United States, he remains celebrated as a player and club maker and is listed among the first 40 golf professionals in the history of the country.

Chapter 13

1909: Georgina 'Jeannie' Burnett

When the Olive Bank Colliery employees of the Niddrie and Benhar Coal Company began work on Wednesday 15th September 1909, little did they realise the events that would unfold there. The colliery site, which operated as a coal depot, was bleak and deserted, surrounded by trees, wasteland and the broken-down high walls that once encircled Olive Bank House. Despite its isolated locale, the depot was remarkably close to the main thoroughfare of Musselburgh, at the west end of Fisherrow near to the High Street, which opened on to the electric tram line.

As the morning shift got underway, engineman Wallace Boynes and his colleagues removed the wooden beams covering the pit shaft to enable water to be drawn off, as it had flooded to within 15 feet of the surface. Boynes and the son of the colliery manager Mr Clark were the first to notice a dark brown object floating in the water. When Boynes lowered his bucket for water, it struck the object, ripping the cloth of the coal sack. A wire rope was used to raise the sack to the surface, where it was found to contain a woman's body.

The discovery was reported to the Musselburgh authorities, and the police began their investigation immediately, with senior officials coordinating with the constabulary in their search of the crime scene. Grappling hooks were employed to search for evidence in the pit shaft, but this proved to be impractical as the flooded tunnel was over 700 feet deep. When the cursory examination was completed, the body was removed from the coal sack and a piece of a Glasgow newspaper, dated 11th June, was found attached to the victim's abdomen.

Professor Harvey Littlejohn, chair of Medical Jurisprudence at Edinburgh University, conducted a post-mortem examination on17th September. His findings noted that the body was doubled up, and a strong cord had been passed around parts of the corpse to bind the victim's head to her feet. Professor Littlejohn believed that the victim had been in the pit shaft for up to three months and was dead before being placed into the sack. The fracture of the thigh and lacerated wound to the skull probably occurred after death. Decomposition of the body meant that a definitive cause of death could not be established – Littlejohn also believed that the internal organs did not reveal any cause of death.

For avoidance of morbid curiosity, the funeral of the victim was organised expeditiously. No mourners attended as the hearse left the mortuary at Musselburgh Town Hall bound for Inveresk churchyard on the afternoon of Saturday 18th September, and no clergyman was present to eulogise the victim, who was interred in a pauper's grave. Unfortunately, the burial proved premature – an exhumation was carried out the following day to allow for formal identification by two landladies who knew the deceased.

However, several days passed before an official statement was issued identifying the victim as Ms Georgina 'Jeannie' Burnett, also known as 'Dundee Doddy'.[8] It was established that Ms Burnett was 26 years of age when she died, and about five feet two inches in height, with a stout build, short black hair, and a perfect set of natural teeth. When she left her lodging house for the last time, she was wearing a thin green straw hat with a pink ribbon, a green motor vale, a wine-coloured costume with a bolero jacket, brown stockings, and brown boots, which had been blackened.

James Hayward, a sailor who had served in the Royal Navy, was quick to make himself known to the authorities and helped to establish Jeannie's movements in the last months of her life. After being discharged from his duties aboard H.M.S. *Agamemnon* on 5th April, Hayward encountered Jeannie outside the Empire Theatre on his first night in Edinburgh. They quickly established a relationship, taking up residence together at different addresses across the city. On Friday 11th June, they engaged rooms as a married couple at 4 East Adam Street in the Pleasance area of the city. They had resided at the property for only a few days when the landlady, Mrs Craig, became dissatisfied with them as tenants. On 14th June, she gave them notice to quit.

Three days later, at about one o'clock in the afternoon, Jeannie left the lodging house, telling Hayward that she was going to Musselburgh to visit an old friend. When Jeannie failed to return, Hayward decided that she must have spent the night with her sister, an opinion he shared with Mrs Craig. However, the deceased's sister, Mrs Knowles, who

---

[8] Doddy: a Scottish term used to describe someone humorously or contemptuously.

lived at 17 East Thomas Street in the city, later advised the police that she not seen her sister since early June. By the next day, Hayward had become anxious and began actively searching for Jeannie, even calling at the local police station and Calton Jail, but to no avail.

As the days after the grim discovery passed by, further details of Jeannie's life emerged. She was the youngest of four children and had stayed with her family in Alexander Street within the Maxwelltown area of Dundee for several years during her adolescence, although the family originated from Aberdeen. Jeannie's father was a pedlar by profession, while her mother was employed in the nearby Caldrum Works. Jeannie attended St Salvador's School, where she displayed a particular aptitude for singing and dancing. Following her mother's death, Jeannie gave up factory work and left Dundee to work in an Edinburgh shop, where she acquitted herself very well.

Nonetheless, she decided to focus on a different career path. Jeannie made a name for herself as a performer, and a Miss Jeannie Burnett is documented as singing as part of a concert party for the South Leith Poorhouse in March 1902. However, her most notable appearances were at the Edinburgh Carnival, held every Christmas at the Waverley Market. She was popular and described as a 'singing mill girl' – a reference to Dundee and the jute industry synonymous with the city.

On the morning of Saturday 25th September, the courthouse at Musselburgh was far busier than usual, local interest piqued by an upcoming appearance before the magistrate by the two men associated with the Burnett case. As the court got underway, Alexander Bisset (42) of Niddrie Cottages, New Craighall, was quickly set free. At eleven o'clock, Mr John Bell (32), employed as night foreman at

New Craighall Pit and resident at North High Street, Musselburgh, was placed in the dock. Described as a well-built man, Bell nonchalantly entered the courtroom, curling his thick moustache as he passed the spectators. With court proceedings underway, the clerk formally requested that Mr Bell should be remanded in custody – a petition that the magistrate duly accepted.

Two days later, John Bell appeared in the dock before the judicial officer, Baillie Kelt,[9] in the Musselburgh Police Court. The burgh public prosecutor explained to the magistrate that the prisoner was in custody in connection with the Olive Bank mystery and asked that he be remitted to the sheriff court. Bell was conveyed to the Midlothian County Police Office in Edinburgh and then on to the sheriff courthouse, before being brought before Sheriff Orr at a private proceeding, where he was committed to prison. Bell spent a month incarcerated in jail but, without enough evidence for a criminal prosecution, he was released.

A Fatal Accident Inquiry under the terms of the (Scotland) Act was conducted by the Procurator Fiscal Mr Renton on Monday 25th October before Sheriff Orr and a jury in Edinburgh's Sheriff Court. Mr Shield appeared on behalf of John Bell, who sat in the well of the court. During the inquiry Alexander Bisset (formerly the co-accused), a surface foreman at New Craighall Pit, gave evidence that Bell had appeared at the pit at five o'clock in the afternoon on Thursday 17th June, when he was due to start work, in the company of a woman.[10] Bell introduced the woman as 'My

---

[9] A bailie or baillie is a civic officer in the local government of Scotland. The position arose in the burghs, where bailies formerly held posts similar to those of aldermen or magistrates.

[10] Bisset identified the woman from a photograph as the deceased Georgina Burnett.

cousin, Miss Burnett, from Dundee', and stated that she had arrived to keep house for him and his invalid aunt. Bell proceeded to show Jeannie around the colliery, and, as they were leaving, informed Bisset that they were going to Portobello.

At around eight o'clock that evening, Bisset met up with the couple in Portobello, and they enjoyed a few drinks together in a public house. At ten o'clock, Bisset saw the pair board a tram at the top of Bath Street, Portobello, and assumed that they were both going to Musselburgh, as he knew that Bell lived in that area. Bisset next saw the accused on the Sunday evening when he came to work, having missed his Friday shift. Neither man had discussed Jeannie, but the witness admitted to the court that he had heard gossip that Jeannie had gone to Brighton to live.

Among the witnesses to appear was Detective Inspector Donald Finlay, who gave evidence relating to Bell's apprehension. On 25th September, Finlay quizzed Bell and asked him if he wished to make a statement. Bell told the Inspector that he had known Jeannie Burnett for about ten years, first meeting her in the Greenmarket area of Dundee while he was attached to a summer camp of the Voluntary Artillery Corps.

Bell then indicated that, on 17th June, quite by accident, he met Burnett in Bath Street, Portobello. They decided to renew their acquaintance and proceeded to Musselburgh and then on to New Craighall Pit. At this juncture, Bell's story follows Bisset's information almost verbatim. However, Bell stated that after he and Jeannie boarded the tramcar on Bath Street at the end of the evening, they alighted before they reached Joppa. To alleviate the argument that ensued, Bell asserted that he produced a pint of whisky, which they then shared. Bell stated that they parted after this – Jeannie taking a tram back to Edinburgh while he continued to Musselburgh.

Detective Inspector Finlay stated that he had completed a comprehensive inquiry amongst the tram conductors of Joppa and Edinburgh but none reported seeing Jeannie travel up to the city. Bell was called back into the witness box and asked if his statement to Detective Inspector Finlay was correct. He replied that it was and that he did not wish to explain himself further.

James Hayward and Professor Littlejohn also appeared as witnesses and provided detailed evidence, as attested to previously, while the depot engineman Wallace Boynes and the colliery manager Mr Clark set out the circumstances of the body's discovery. The landlady Mrs Craig, who helped with formal identification of the victim's body, reiterated that she saw Jeannie on the day of her disappearance as she departed the lodging house. Mr Alexander Webster, a tobacconist by trade and an early example of an expert witness, was called by the inquiry and stated that the cord used to tie up the victim was similar to items he sold as fishing tackle. Mary Johnston, employed at a laundry in St John's Street, Edinburgh, frequented by the victim, reported that certain marks found on the victim's undergarments were produced as part of the laundry process.

In Mr Renton's final directions, he stated that it was necessary under the terms of Scottish law that the jury determine the victim's date of death or as close an approximation to it as the evidence would allow. He reiterated that the circumstances surrounding the discovery of Ms Burnett's body pointed very strongly to foul play, yet there was no tangible evidence to bring charges against anyone.

The fatal accident inquiry into the death of Jeannie Burnett reached several conclusions. It was agreed that the victim's body had been found in Olive Bank Pit, Musselburgh, at around two o'clock on 15th September, and that the victim had last seen alive in Portobello at about ten o'clock on the night of 17th June. While the coroner, Professor Littlejohn, believed that the victim was dead before entering the sack, it was not possible to establish a definitive cause of death and no evidence showed that anyone was involved with or contributed to the death of Ms Burnett.

The story of Georgina 'Jeannie' Burnett disappeared from the public gaze as quickly as it had arrived – no solution was found and no charges were filed. If the fatal accident inquiry had not taken place, no coherent timeline to the case or to Jeannie's life would have been put in place. However, several months after the inquiry, in April 1910, John Bell appeared before the magistrate in Musselburgh. Mr Bell, of no fixed abode, was charged with robbery, having stolen, among other items, two rings and a pair of earrings from his disabled aunt. Asked for his petition to the court, Mr Bell stated that he had lost his job and could not get any form of employment in the Musselburgh area. In reply, the judicial officer Baillie Miller described the case as 'contemptible' and imposed a sentence of 60 days in prison.

Chapter 14

1913: The Gosford Gamekeeper

Gosford House is a neoclassical mansion situated in some 5,000 acres of rolling parkland and undulating coastline about two miles northeast of Longniddry. The property was one of the last commissions of the renowned Scottish architect Robert Adam, completed in 1800 under the stewardship of the 7th Earl of Wemyss. Over 100 years later, the estate came under the spotlight not for a high society marriage or newly established political career involving one of the Charteris family but for the actions of a trusted and respected gamekeeper.

John and Elizabeth Saunders married on 24th May 1901 and enjoyed a somewhat disjointed married life over the subsequent 12 years. By the beginning of 1913, Elizabeth Saunders (37) displayed all the hallmark symptoms of anxiety, leaving her prone to bouts of dyspepsia, melancholy and panic attacks. The household at their marital home, Gosford West Lodge, included the gamekeeper, his overwrought wife, her elderly mother and the couple's 21-year-old niece, Mary Douglas Chirnside. The home become a stagnant environment to live in, and the childless marriage had resulted in a stale situation, with Elizabeth prone to outbursts of anger interlaced with bouts of illness, while John focused on working hard at his gamekeeping job.

During John's free time, he would regularly shoot at the range between Hareston Wood and Craigielaw Point as a reserve member of the 4th (Aberlady) Corps of the Haddingtonshire Rifle Volunteers, mainly made up of Gosford Estate staff. Unfortunately, Elizabeth objected to her husband's busy life, and, while she was genuinely worried about his safety, especially as he worked a night shift, and given the threat that poachers presented to gamekeepers, she also considered the spectre of infidelity too.

John Saunders began to openly complain about the increasingly strained state of his marriage. He could not reconcile himself with the ever-increasing expenditure of the household on food and felt that the presence of his wife's niece resulted from pure vanity – in his mind, Elizabeth was very capable of doing the daily chores herself. By January 1913, events had taken a distinctly sinister turn, and, on the 17th of the month, Elizabeth was enjoying her usual breakfast tray in bed when she became aware of a 'nasty bitter taste' on her toast. As the days progressed, she encountered this same vile taste more frequently and thought that the gas cinders used to heat the toast created a particularly odd aftertaste.

By Wednesday 22nd January, Elizabeth had begun to feel faint and nauseous and decided to take a mixture of bicarbonate of soda and hot water to induce vomiting. This process appeared to settle her symptoms, but the very next day, a more perplexing set of events occurred. After eating some toast and drinking some tea, which had an intense acerbic taste, Elizabeth was suddenly overcome – her leg muscles became numb, and her body went into an involuntary spasm. She began to choke and was forced to grab the nape of her own neck with her hand. The upper set of her false teeth came out, and the rigidity in her jaw forced her lower teeth to become fixed in her upper gums.

Hearing Elizabeth's distress, her young niece Mary came to her aid and gripped her prone figure through three attacks until she vomited, which appeared to relieve her suffering. In genuine concern for her aunt's wellbeing, Mary telegraphed immediately for medical assistance. Unfortunately, their usual physician, Dr Millar from Tranent, was unavailable, so he sent his assistant, Dr Gamble. When the practitioner arrived in the evening, he found a woman not suffering from any physical illness but highly emotionally disturbed.

Despite prescribing bromide for this perceived nervous affliction, the next morning, Dr Millar made a house call. He had ministered to Mrs Saunders's medical needs for over seven years and was familiar with her case history and her propensity to complain. He noted that she had a pallid look about her and had endured a 'bad turn' but thought her protestations that she had been poisoned were pure fantasy. Nonetheless, Dr Millar advised that a resident nurse should be employed.

Elizabeth Cameron was duly installed as a nurse at Gosford West Lodge on Friday 24th January. She was eminently qualified for her new position as she had already nursed Mrs Saunders during a previous illness. Over the following two weeks, Nurse Cameron proved to be a diligent caregiver, insisting on total bed rest and taking the time to listen to the thoughts and feelings of her patient. As the days passed, Nurse Cameron also investigated the contents of the kitchen cupboard and on tasting the marmalade she found it very bitter. She provided a sample to the doctor, but the marmalade jar had been replaced with a new one by the time of his return visit. However, Nurse Cameron's amateur sleuthing also revealed that wheaten biscuits had been tampered with, while the cream in the bottle was positively sour on two separate occasions.

By 8th February, Elizabeth had regained some of her strength and was out of bed. Nurse Cameron and Mrs Saunders' niece, Mary Chirnside, were encouraged by this development, and the nurse gave some cream from a newly delivered bottle to her patient. Breakfast passed without incident, but, when the nurse, accompanied by Mary, examined the new bottle some two hours later, they found it to have a bitter taste. The gravity of the situation forced Nurse Cameron to give the remainder of the bottle to Dr Millar, to whom she communicated her fears.

Dr Millar contacted the police directly over Nurse Cameron's growing suspicions, and Professor Harvey Littlejohn and Dr Sydney Smith of Edinburgh University undertook a full analysis of the samples supplied. The results showed that the wheaten biscuit, marmalade and spoilt cream contained around 21 milligrams of strychnine, a dosage that was not ordinarily fatal but was extremely dangerous and could, in certain circumstances, induce death. John Saunders was arrested and taken into custody, but, on searching the property, no strychnine was discovered. The accused could not be linked to any purchase of the highly toxic poison despite the alkaloid being the chosen pesticide utilised by gamekeepers.

By the time Lord Ormidale opened legal proceedings against John Saunders on 23rd April 1913 at the High Court of Justiciary in Edinburgh, a growing fascination with the accused had developed on the part of the media and the general public. Saunders stood in the dock charged with administering poison to his wife Elizabeth with intent to murder. This assertion had resulted in a crowded gallery, with spectators eager to follow the case.

Saunders did not conform to perceived ideas of what a poisoner should look like. In pre-First World War society, a gender bias endured to suggest that nearly all poisoners were female, with celebrated Victorian cases such as Mary Ann Cotton and Florence Maybrick still fresh in the public memory. When the gamekeeper appeared before the court and entered a plea of not guilty, he displayed a genial manner that, coupled with his fresh complexion and tall, well-built frame, helped to reinforce a favourable impression in the eyes of the jury.

As the prosecution case got underway, Elizabeth Saunders was questioned by the Solicitor General of Scotland, Andrew Anderson K.C., giving her the opportunity to put forward a clear and concise narrative. However, the defence cross-examination was a far more onerous process. Mr Wilson K.C. diligently probed the witness on her physical and mental health. The reasoning behind this line of questioning was to establish whether Mrs Saunders had a fear of being poisoned, although she never agreed that this was the case.

It emerged that, earlier in her married life, Elizabeth Saunders had suffered a breakdown after accidentally poisoning herself. Inadvertently, she took a dessert spoon of Easton's syrup, which contained strychnine, instead of a teaspoonful. As the cross-examination continued, Elizabeth Saunders denied that she had told Dr Millar and Nurse Cameron that she believed she was being poisoned. She categorically denied that in 1912 she had told her husband that 'someday he would find her down in the sea' or that she had asserted that she 'would have been poisoned long ago if the doctor had not been looking after her'.

Elizabeth Saunders admitted that she was unhappy with her life at Gosford and had actively encouraged her husband to consider a move away to pursue a brighter future for them both. John Saunders disagreed and felt that they had a good life working on the Gosford Estate. During the trial, Mrs Saunders stated that she had received a visit from a Dundee solicitor, who informed her that a great uncle of hers had died in Australia, leaving a large fortune of which she was a beneficiary. Neither the prosecution nor defence counsel attempted to quantify her assertions to establish their accuracy.

As Dr Gamble provided his statement to the court, he admitted that he had diagnosed symptoms that he could not quantify while attending Mrs Saunders. He stated that the patient revealed to him 'that she was afraid of something coming over her, and she lacked the willpower to conquer it'. She later alluded to a friend who had drowned herself and asked him if any possibility existed that she might do something to herself.

Dr Millar testified that Mrs Saunders was a nervous patient, and that, in such cases, symptoms could be imagined. In his opinion, if the individual who put 'the poison on the biscuit meant it to be consumed by somebody else, he went very poorly about his business: the thing was so apparent'. This admission by the general practitioner most associated with Mrs Saunders' healthcare could not help but benefit the case for the defence. Under cross-examination, Dr Millar admitted to the defence that he had never known such a low dosage of strychnine to prove to be fatal.

After Nurse Cameron's powerful testimony relating to the tainted food discovery, she was asked under cross-examination about her previous dealings with Mrs Saunders, primarily concerning her earlier illness in 1912. She told the court that Mrs Saunders was predisposed to vivid and frightening dreams and was deeply unhappy at Gosford. She would get up at odd hours during the night when Mr Saunders was at work on the estate, disconcerted by feelings of doom about her husband's safety.

The defence case that followed included a litany of medical professionals, who put forward convoluted arguments about Elizabeth Saunders' mental health. It was reasoned that she fabricated strychnine poisoning to preserve the status quo of her home – so that her niece and mother could continue to reside at Gosford West Lodge and to curtail her husband from staying out late at night.

This was described as the act of a desperate woman driven to seek attention but who had not openly planned her subterfuge – instead, events unfolded at an unconscious level. As part of the expert medical evidence, Dr George Lovell Gulland stated that, while he had been treating Mrs Saunders in Chalmers Hospital, Edinburgh, in February and March 1906, he became aware that the patient was prone to hypochondria and 'sat on the borderland between sanity and insanity'.

Dr Sillar provided expert pharmacological evidence about the samples, although the Crown case failed to drive home any succinct points in their favour. When later questioned about the mental state of Mrs Saunders, he declined to give a definitive opinion, nor did he reveal whether Mrs Saunders would have died if she had consumed the poison in other food in the house.

The eminent Scottish psychiatrist Sir Thomas Clouston, whose appointments included physician superintendent of the Royal Asylum and lecturer on mental diseases at the University of Edinburgh, also gave his respected opinion. Clouston did not carry out an examination of Elizabeth

Saunders but indicated his belief in 'the probability or possibility that she used strychnine on the articles of food herself to excite sympathy'.

Clouston conceded that he could not state that Mrs Saunders displayed signs of neuroses while she was in the witness box, but he cautioned the court that those afflicted with hysteria were more than capable of acting rationally. Clouston further noted that Elizabeth Saunders had a self-congratulatory look on her face as she left the witness box, testimony which was later derided. However, for a partisan gallery and a jury comprised solely of men, such words were damaging to the prosecution's case and sewed inevitable seeds of doubt.

When John Saunders took to the stand, the defence barrister gave him the same opportunity afforded to Elizabeth by the prosecution – in this case, he put forward a simple submission that he was the innocent party and that his wife was prone to suicidal tendencies. Saunders claimed that his wife Elizabeth had stated on several occasions throughout their marriage that she would do something to herself.

He recounted an event when his wife Elizabeth had left their home to go down to the shoreline and confirmed that his mother-in-law had asked him to follow. Less than three quarters of a mile from home, his wife promptly turned around and returned home. The following day, in a frivolous manner, he asked, 'What if the water had been too cold?'

She replied, 'I will do it one day.'

John Saunders denied that he had any real problems in his marriage with the exception of his wife's temper tantrums. He conceded that she could 'fix on certain things, especially when she heard about a suicide'. After tasting the allegedly tainted marmalade, Saunders conceded that it had a pungent smell, and caused a burning sensation in his throat.

Despite this, he did not inform his wife as he believed that she was plotting with the intention of apportioning blame on him.

The prosecution counsel's closing arguments stated that the Crown's case had shown that 'human agency' had been used to add 'strychnine to Mrs Saunders' food to poison her'. In addition, the Solicitor General submitted that 'the chain of circumstances was complete, and that the crime was clearly and satisfactorily proven'. Mr Wilson, for the defence, countered that the 'case was not who put the strychnine in the food' but rather, 'had the Crown proved that the prisoner had done so'. He further noted that, because of the complexities of the trial, 'at the end of the day, it may be left more or less in mystery'.

The trial judge Lord Ormidale addressed the jury, stating that the 'burden of proof was on the Crown', and therefore he asked that they did not balance one theory against the other. Evidence to suggest any motive on the part of the prisoner was arguably lacking. It was for them to consider whether John Saunders was so skilful under the cloak of his excellent character to plan to take the life of his wife. The jury retired to consider the case put before them.

The prosecution had manfully put forward a hypothesis that John Saunders had actively endeavoured to kill his wife by means of strychnine poisoning. The defence countered this with theories that Elizabeth Saunders possessed the necessary medical knowledge to take a strychnine dosage that would result in the necessary symptoms without proving fatal. An alternate hypothesis had even suggested that Mrs Saunders had ingested the poison on several occasions as she suffered from ongoing suicidal tendencies.

The jury took less than three quarters of an hour to complete their final analysis and return a unanimous verdict of not guilty. In a future twist of fate, Lord Ormidale once again presided over Mr and Mrs Saunders, this time in their divorce proceedings granting a decree in favour of the husband on the grounds of spousal desertion.

Chapter 15

1922: Without a Shred of Evidence

The arrival of the 1920s in Scotland heralded a new sense of promise and optimism as people looked to consign the tragedies of the First World War to living memory. It was an era of modern technology, from the advent of electric refrigerators to the development of automobiles and the radio. In the grocery sector, food processing advanced significantly with the arrival of canned and frozen foods. However, the daily activities of Helen Blackie (69) as a shopkeeper in rural East Lothian had changed little in nearly 30 years of business.

On Tuesday 11th April 1922, the elderly spinster's day began – she rose as usual before six o'clock in the morning to prepare to open up her small shop. In the small hamlet of Meadowmill, famed as the field on which the Battle of Prestonpans was fought in 1745, the elderly spinster ran a thriving grocery and ale business. As she opened for business just before eight o'clock that morning, nearby residents noticed two men enter the store. By midday, when Mr Lees, the delivery man from the nearby Haddington Brewery, arrived, he was surprised to find Miss Blackie's business quiet.

The house occupied by Miss Blackie was a two-storey property. Part of the ground floor was home to the shop, and the upper floor acted as a dwelling house. When Miss Blackie failed to respond to his verbal greetings, Mr Lees entered the property, thinking that perhaps she was in the back garden. On gaining access, however, he was horrified to find Miss Blackie lying on her face in the lobby in a pool of blood, with a terrible gaping wound at the back of her head. A commonplace joiner's claw hammer was lying close by, covered in blood.

Mr Lees quickly raised the alarm, and Inspector Gray from Tranent arrived at the murder scene. The victim was found to have suffered several wounds to the back of her head, and the post-mortem examination concluded that a laceration to the brain and excessive blood loss resulted in death. Suspicion quickly fell upon the men who had visited the shop, and Duncan Carmichael (25) and David Drummond (40) were interviewed by sheriff substitute Mr Wilson before being taken into custody.

As the community came to terms with the savage murder that had taken place in their midst, a sombre but respectful funeral took place for Helen Blackie on Thursday 13th April 1922, conducted by the Rev. Howat, minister of Tranent Parish Church. The deceased's nephews, Mr William Harrison and Mr James Harrison, were present. A single wreath lay on the black coffin, and around 50 mourners attended the funeral as Helen Blackie was interred next to her parents in the shadow of the churchyard walls.

As time progressed, the apparent lack of motive for the killing became of growing importance to the authorities and the general public. The police had been working on the hypothesis that robbery motivated the murder, but further investigations showed that it could not be established whether money had been taken. The till was empty except for some two shillings in copper coins, but the police discovered money in the victim's house. The detained men were finally brought before the court on Tuesday 16th May 1922, indicted for murder.

It emerged that Helen Blackie's neighbours, including her nephews, who lived in the adjoining property, had heard nothing untoward on the morning of the murder. Police inquiries revealed that the victim was last seen alive when she took down the shop's shutters that morning. In passing through the lobby of the property, Helen must have met the intruder – her body lay where she was struck with a hammer that usually sat on the shop counter, where it was used to open packages and boxes.

When the murder trial got underway at the High Court, Edinburgh, on Thursday 20th July 1922, the accused men had been in custody for over three months. Appearing before Lord Anderson, both entered pleas of not guilty to the charge of murdering Miss Helen Blackie at her property in Meadowmill. The Hon. William Watson K.C., Solicitor General, and Lord Kinross, Advocate-Depute, conducted the Crown case, while Mr Mackay, K.C. and Mr Gibb appeared for the defence. Over 50 witnesses were requested to appear in the case, meaning that it proved time-consuming and financially costly to prepare.

James Anderson, a roadworker, was one of the first witnesses to appear. He stated that, on the morning of the murder and while working on the road between Prestonpans station and Meadowmill, he encountered two men at between seven o'clock and eight o'clock in the morning. Anderson stated that he heard one of the men saying to his companion, 'Paddy, I could do with two duck eggs and a slice of bacon for breakfast this morning.' He identified the accused as the two men he saw, further noting that they journeyed on towards Meadowmill.

Murray Mackenzie (11) stated that he was outside playing on the morning in question when he observed Miss Blackie looking out of the window of her house. He saw one of the men pointing to the shop door, and Miss Blackie opened it. The witness indicated that the two men left the shop about five minutes later, carrying a parcel of ham, before going next door to Mrs Graham, who fried the ham for them. The boy was hesitant to identify the accused but told the court that the two men were the ones he had seen.

Mr Lees, who discovered the victim's body, recounted his statement that he had provided to the police, and noted shocking circumstances of the incident. Following the cross-examination by the defence barrister Mr Mackay, the Solicitor General stated that it was his duty, after hearing the testimony from Mr Lees, to withdraw the Crown charge against the two men.

In his opinion, it was essential to the case that, as the murder was discovered at noon, it was necessary to prove that the shop door was closed when the two accused men left the shop. Given Murray Mackenzie's evidence, it would have been impossible for the Crown case to maintain that the shop door was closed until the body was found.

In less than two hours, the case against Duncan Carmichael and David Drummond lay in tatters, and Lord Anderson was quick to vilify the authorities for what he believed was complete ineptitude. He stated that evidence pointed very clearly to the innocence of the two accused men: 'one did not see so far as the evidence has gone any justification on the part of the police for bringing these men into the dock.' He therefore saw it as his duty to see that the accused men were discharged from court, instructing the jury to return a formal verdict of not guilty.

In the aftermath of the debacle, the police found themselves no further forward in the hunt for Helen Blackie's killer, while the trial's ramifications led to public outcry and calls for an official inquiry. The case turned into a minor cause célèbre, and Mr William Murray, the solicitor who conducted the defence case, was quick to champion his clients' cause. From Murray's investigations and information discerned from the police, he believed that there was never any vestige of evidence against them.

The accused had been kept in prison for 100 days – almost up to the limit set in the Scots *Habeas Corpus Act* (110 days) for the time someone could be held before being brought to trial. The prosecution failed to supply any evidence to justify the indictment made against them or their long detention. Murray noted that, 'I never came across anything so absurd in my life.' Expanding on how the defence case had developed, the barrister detailed his first encounter with his clients in the sheriff court at Haddington. He remembered that he looked at them and remarked, 'You are a bonnie pair to have killed an old lady.'

The elder of the two men, Drummond, said, 'Do we look like murderers, Sir?' They provided Murray with a comprehensive account, stating that they had only met the evening before the murder at a brickworks at Prestongrange. They struck up an easy accord and, as they were both travelling east in search of work, decided to make the journey together.

On the following morning, they arrived in the hamlet of Meadowmill and went into the shop to purchase some bacon, which they took next door to be cooked while Drummond went to get some bread. They ate their hearty breakfast and travelled on towards Haddington, where a young lad told them that a woman had been murdered. They were surprised to hear this news but continued travelling on to Haddington, where they were met by the police. Carmichael and Drummond had only two pence between them when they arrived in Haddington – the remains of the shilling they had used to buy their breakfast.

Murray revealed that an analyst from Edinburgh carried out a thorough examination of the men's clothes but found no trace of blood on any of their garments. Each man was allegedly offered immunity from prosecution if they agreed to give evidence against the other. On one of the last occasions when the accused men went before Sheriff MacLeod, Murray protested against the return of his clients to prison. However, the Procurator Fiscal stated that he could not liberate the accused without sanction from the Crown counsel.

Murray believed that blame for the case lay with the Crown authorities and not with police observation of due diligence in reporting the facts of the case. Even the jury foreman Mr Kelso Kelly noted that the evidence against the men represented a woeful display of shreds and patches, describing it as 'incoherent, confused and useless, save that it tended more to support the evidence favouring the accused men than to establish their guilt'.

In the House of Commons, Mr. P.J. Ford, member of parliament for North Edinburgh, endeavoured to call attention to the long detention of the accused, asking what reparations were being offered to the two men and, if no reparations were due, whether it was proposed to introduce legislation to remedy the problem. In response, the Secretary of State for Scotland, Robert Munro, stated, 'According to general practice in such cases, no compensation is awarded. I see no official reason to make an exception in the case mentioned, nor do I think legislation is required.'

In the weeks that followed, the murder investigation ground to a complete halt. No new suspects came to light and the victim's killer was never identified or tried for murder. When the private estate of Helen Blackie was assessed by the solicitors of Fraser and Maitland, they noted that the deceased had over £3,500 in savings and, taken in total with various bonds, shares and personal effects, her estate was worth £4,463: 8: 6d – equivalent to a quarter of a million pounds today. On 18th July 1922, Helen Blackie's bachelor nephew James Harrison took possession of his aunt's estate under deposition oath and remained in Meadowmill for the next 32 years until his death in 1954.

Chapter 16

1940: A Crime of Passion

Within the county of East Lothian, few coastal towns have as rich and diverse a history as Dunbar. The name itself is derived from the ancient Celtic language of Brythonic, and the words 'Dyn barr' translate as 'the fort of the point' A stronghold was established on the site by the kingdom of Bernicia in the 7th century, as the headland represented a particularly suitable location to ward off attacks from land or sea.

Over the following centuries, the area featured heavily in the turbulent affairs of our island nation, as was perhaps most vividly demonstrated in 1338. In January of that year, the Countess of Douglas, known as 'Black Agnes', managed to defend Dunbar Castle against the Earl of Salisbury's English forces with the help of only a few servants, guards and loyal townsfolk. Such was their success that, after a five-month stalemate, the invaders were forced to withdraw, handing the Countess a defining victory.

By 1370 Dunbar had become a royal burgh and, as Scotland and England continued to control the castle and town, the town grew slowly. Consequently, the area continued to feature in major military engagements such as the Battle of Dunbar (1650), when Oliver Cromwell's parliamentarians routed the army of the Scottish Covenanters. By the time of the Napoleonic Wars, soldiers were billeted in the town centre and in camps positioned on the beach. In 1855 Lauderdale House was acquired by the War Office, and Castle Park Barracks was formally established as home to the 1st Haddingtonshire Artillery Volunteers. The barracks played an essential role during the First World War, continuing to provide up-to-date accommodation for army units. By the time of the Second World War, Lauderdale House had become the headquarters of the 165th Officer Training Unit, tasked with marshalling the town's defence against German invasion.

Despite Dunbar's long association with the military, which provided much welcome economic support, the area is also a well-known centre of agricultural excellence. In addition, the port sustained a healthy herring industry and was home to high levels of boat-building activity well into the 20th century. This diverse range of professions in turn facilitated a cross-section of religious worship that included Roman Catholicism, Wesleyan, United Associate Synod and Free Church activity. Perhaps appropriately, therefore, this case takes account of two factors predominantly associated with Dunbar, namely Black Agnes' passion in her defence of Dunbar Castle and the proud military tradition of the town, which stretches back into antiquity.

When the trial began against Alexander Norval McWilliam (34) at the High Court in Edinburgh on 5th November 1940, the court had little awareness of the crime of passion that had taken place. The charge asserted that Mr McWilliam had murdered his wife, Elizabeth McWilliam (26), known as Betty to her friends, at their home at 5 Boroughdales, Dunbar, on 1st September 1940. As the case unfolded, it emerged that the death of Mrs McWilliam was particularly ferocious, yet this was a tragedy that had engulfed a whole family.

Alexander Norval McWilliam and Elizabeth Robertson married in 1931 and enjoyed a happy and contented marriage in the subsequent nine years. Mr McWilliam worked as a painter, and the Bo'ness native was a loving husband to his wife and father to their three young children. By September 1940, though, the family dynamic had changed. Alexander spent six months training as a gunner with the Royal Artillery while his wife worked as a hairdresser, taking in lodgers to help make ends meet. Sunday 1st September 1940 started promptly for the family, with Alexander and Betty attending church with their children. After the service, the family visited Betty's mother and enjoyed a pleasant lunch with her.

When Alexander McWilliam took to the stand, he outlined, in hushed tones, that he had come across a letter in his wife's handbag by chance later that same afternoon. When he began to read the correspondence, he immediately noticed the intimate terms used, such as 'My darling' and 'I love you', stating that, he therefore 'went a bit off [his] head'. He related that he had challenged his wife about the letter and told her to leave.

At his behest, Mrs McWilliam picked up her handbag and coat, but Mr McWilliam decided that he wanted to continue the conversation. The situation escalated and, in a locked bedroom, he carried out the fatal attack on his wife. He noted to the court that he had no recollection of getting hold of a hatchet or the frequency with which he struck his wife. All he could remember was 'catching hold of her and striking her'. He then left the room via the window, travelled down to the rocks, slipped, and fell into the water. Subsequently, he sat quietly for a long time before regaining possession of his senses.

Sir George Morton K.C., representing the defence, asked his client, 'Is it the case that your mind was a complete blank about the happenings after you discovered that letter until sometime after you left the house?'

Mr McWilliam replied, 'All I could remember was that I had done something.' During the Crown's cross-examination, undertaken by Mr L. Hill Watson K.C., the accused stated that he did not remember talking to a female lodger who had asked him not to break up his home, to whom he allegedly replied, 'My home was broken up long ago.'

Lord Aitchison then interceded in the proceedings, asking, 'When you told your wife to get out of the house, did she ask you why?' Mr McWilliam replied that she had not.

'Did she seem to understand why she was being put out?' enquired Lord Aitchison.

The accused replied, 'I think she understood.'

Taking to the stand, the mother of the victim, Mrs Elizabeth Robertson of 17 Victoria Street, Dunbar, stated, that since her daughter's marriage, the couple had been happy together and raised three children – a boy aged 8 and girls aged 7 and 4. Unfortunately, in her opinion, this happy home life had changed in recent months. The witness confirmed that her daughter was on friendly terms with a man named Sergeant Sharp.

Mrs Norah Matheson then took to the stand, stating that the deceased had given her some private letters for safe keeping. Mrs McWilliam had intimated that the letters were from her brother. Mrs Matheson's daughter also took to the witness stand to give a vivid account of the events of that Sunday afternoon in her capacity as a lodger with the family. Mrs Kate Florence Maskell declared that she had seen a marked difference in Alexander McWilliam's character after he came home on leave. Mrs Maskell stated that Mrs

McWilliam had gone into the bedroom to talk with her husband and returned in a bad temper. She confided to Mrs Maskell that, 'Mac [referring to her husband] has been through my handbag and told me to get out, and I am getting out.'

Mrs Maskell reported that, 'A few minutes later, just after Betty had left the room for a second time, I heard a noise. I turned off the radio, and I heard two more bangs. I thought something had happened and knocked on the door. I never heard another sound but knew something had happened, so I sent for help.'

Private Percival Franklin testified that he lived with his family in a house above that of the accused. At about four o'clock in the afternoon, he reported hearing 'four distinct thuds from the room directly below'. He said that he remarked to his wife, 'There goes the happy home.' Almost immediately afterwards, Mrs Maskell arrived and asked him to check on Mrs McWilliam. When he attempted to do so, he found the bedroom window open and heard faint moans. Looking in the window, he reported seeing 'the lower half of a woman's body on the floor', upon which he immediately called the police.

Constable Edward Kell of East Lothian Constabulary supplied police evidence and detailed the transfer of the victim to Dunbar Cottage Hospital, where she died from her injuries on 4th September 1940. During Constable Kell's preliminary search of the property, he identified a small hatchet in the bedroom, which was confirmed as the murder weapon. Additional information was supplied by Inspector William Johnston, who detailed the correspondence between Elizabeth McWilliam and Sergeant Alf Sharp.

A handful of letters were recovered, which included expressions of endearment and proposed assignations between Mrs McWilliam and Sergeant Sharp. Sharp stated in one letter that he was confined to barracks after receiving a District Court Martial, requesting of Mrs McWilliam that she call at the camp to see him. He suggested that she should tell the military police officer on duty that she was his sister. Under cross-examination, Inspector Johnston indicated that he had interviewed Sharp, who admitted to writing the letters and knowing the deceased for nearly two years.

Professor Sydney Smith carried out a post-mortem on the deceased, aided by Dr William Lowe Anderson of Templelands, Dunbar. Professor Smith stated that the cause of death was damage to the brain caused by repeated blows to the head. Five blows had been struck – one on the left side of the head, three on the right temple and another, which had burst open the right eye. In his opinion, the blows could have been inflicted with a hatchet. Dr Anderson admitted to the court in his evidence that the injuries could have been caused by a man who had temporarily lost control of his emotions after hearing of his wife's infidelity.

In a relatively short case by the standards of the day, the summing up process proved particularly eventful. Lord Justice Clerk (Lord Aitchison) was scathing in his comments about Sergeant Alfred Sharp's role in the case, stating that, 'that this lamentable tragedy would never have occurred but for the fact that during the accused's absence on military service another man was trafficking with his wife.'

Lord Aitchison used the expression 'trafficking' but noted that, based on the content of the uncovered letters, he would not have the slightest hesitation in concluding that an improper intimacy existed between Sergeant Sharp and Elizabeth McWilliam. He further stated that Sergeant Sharp should have appeared in the witness box for 'the hefty moral responsibility that rests on the man who came between the accused and his wife'.

Sir George Morton's final remarks for the defence drew the jury's attention to the question of whether the case was one of murder or culpable homicide. He outlined that, if Mr McWilliam had found his wife in the act of adultery or in a situation that showed that adultery had just been committed, the crime would, of course, be classified as culpable homicide. After all, under Scots law, allowance is given for human frailties.

This was not a case of a man who had planned and plotted to murder his wife, and an element of provocation was apparent. The ultimate question was, 'Can the provocation in question be enough to reduce the crime to a lesser charge?' Indeed, evidence suggested that Alexander McWilliam's balance of mind was disturbed during the attack, raising questions about whether the shock was so great that he ceased to be fully responsible for his actions and how, if the balance of his mind was not disturbed, his actions could be accounted for. Indeed, the evidence about his character was that he was a loving husband and father prior to his wife's death.

Enough evidence emerged in the case to justify reducing the charge to culpable homicide. The accused was on leave, on orders to proceed abroad to war, and his wife's conduct might very well have had a profoundly disturbing effect upon his mind. It was recommended that the members of the jury, in making up their mind on a narrow and challenging case, should lean towards mercy.

After only a few minutes of deliberation, the jury returned a unanimous verdict of culpable homicide. In passing sentence on Alexander McWilliam, the Lord Justice Clerk said the accused had used terrible violence against his wife but that he was satisfied that he acted impulsively, without premeditation, and under very considerable provocation. He took into account his excellent character and that he had been a loving father and dutiful husband until the time of the attack. Nonetheless, the severe nature of the crime warranted a sentence of eight years' penal servitude.

Surprisingly, over the last century, Scottish working-class men were nearly 20 percent more likely to be convicted of killing their wives than men from higher socio-economic groups. However, a blue-collar worker convicted of murdering his wife had a far greater chance of receiving a lighter sentence than his white-collar counterpart. In historiographic terms, this centres upon class distinction – more is expected from an upper-class gentleman in adhering to the rule of law, whereas a working-class man is perceived to have indoctrinated failings resulting from a lack of education and therefore a greater propensity to break the law. In short, a lighter sentence for a working-class man might benefit his future behaviour beyond his prison term. A far more sinister idea related to misogyny – arguably, the life of a working-class woman was not considered as important.

Despite the mitigating circumstances surrounding this case, it is reasonable to argue that the judicial system was compassionate in sentencing Alexander McWilliam. Three young children were deprived of both their mother and father, and, thankfully, the culpable homicide charge prevented a murder trial, which could have led to a death sentence for the accused. Less than ten years later, under the terms of the Criminal Justice (Scotland) Act 1949 Section 16(1), penal servitude was abolished in Scotland on 12th June 1950. As for Alexander Norval McWilliam, his criminal case file at the National Records of Scotland is temporarily closed under the NRS reclosure policy.

Printed in Great Britain
by Amazon